Loving Yourself

Empower Yourself, Overcome Trauma

Cathleen R. Barton

Loving Yourself: Empower Yourself, Overcome Trauma

Table of Contents

Book 1 - Empower Yourself

A Comprehensive Guide to Unlocking Your Inner Potential and Achieving Success in Every Area of Your Life Through Self-Discovery, Personal Development, and Mindset Mastery

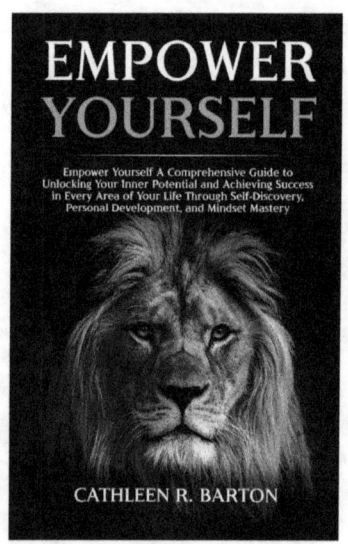

01: Introduction: Unlocking Your Inner Potential

Introduction

We all have the potential to achieve great things, but sometimes it can be difficult to tap into that potential. Whether it's due to self-doubt, fear, or a lack of understanding of our own abilities, unlocking our inner potential can seem like a daunting task. But the truth is, it's not as difficult as we may think. With the right mindset and a few key strategies, anyone can unlock their inner potential and achieve their goals.

First, it's important to understand that our potential is not fixed. We are not limited by our past experiences or our current circumstances. Instead, our potential is constantly evolving and expanding as we learn new things and develop new skills. This means that we have the ability to improve and grow, no matter how old we are or what we've accomplished so far.

One of the key ways to unlock our inner potential is to set clear, specific goals. This means taking the time to think about what we want to achieve, and then breaking that goal down into smaller, actionable steps. This not only helps us to focus our efforts, but it also gives us a sense of direction and purpose, which can be incredibly motivating.

Another important strategy for unlocking our inner potential is to focus on our strengths. We all have unique talents and abilities, and focusing on these strengths can help us to achieve our goals more easily and efficiently. This means taking the time to identify our strengths and then finding ways to use them in our everyday lives, whether that's at work, at home, or in our personal relationships.

Another key strategy for unlocking our inner potential is to be proactive. This means taking control of our own lives and taking steps to achieve our goals, rather than waiting for opportunities to come to us. Being proactive also means being willing to take risks and step out of our comfort zones. It's easy to get stuck in a rut, but taking risks and trying new things can help us to discover new opportunities and unlock our inner potential.

It's also important to build a supportive network of people around us. Whether it's friends, family, or colleagues, having people in our lives who believe in us and support our goals can make a huge difference in our ability to achieve them. These people can provide guidance, encouragement, and a sounding board for our ideas and aspirations.

Finally, one of the most important strategies for unlocking our inner potential is to be open to learning and growth. This means being willing to try new things, make mistakes, and learn from our experiences. We are never done learning and growing, and by embracing this mindset, we can continue to unlock our inner potential and achieve our goals.

In conclusion, unlocking our inner potential is not as difficult as we may think. It's about setting clear, specific goals, focusing on our strengths, being proactive, building a supportive network, and being open to learning and growth. By following these strategies, we can tap into our inner potential and achieve the things we've always dreamed of.

Another important aspect of unlocking our inner potential is self-awareness. Understanding who we are, what motivates us, and what our values and beliefs are is crucial in order to set meaningful and achievable goals. Self-awareness also allows us to identify and overcome limiting beliefs and negative self-talk that may be holding us back.

01: INTRODUCTION: UNLOCKING YOUR INNER PO-TENTIAL

One way to increase self-awareness is through mindfulness practices such as meditation or journaling. These practices can help us to quiet the constant chatter of our minds and tune into our inner selves. This can also give us a deeper understanding of our thoughts, feelings, and behaviors and how they may be impacting our ability to reach our potential.

Another way to increase self-awareness is to seek feedback from others. This could be through a mentor, coach or even a trusted friend or family member. This can provide valuable perspective and insights on areas where we may be holding ourselves back and areas where we excel.

In addition to self-awareness, another important aspect of unlocking our inner potential is self-care. Taking care of our physical, emotional, and mental well-being is crucial in order to be able to perform at our best. This means making sure we are getting enough sleep, eating a healthy diet, and exercising regularly. It also means taking the time to do things that bring us joy and make us feel good, such as spending time with loved ones, reading, or pursuing a hobby.

01: INTRODUCTION: UNLOCKING YOUR INNER PO-
TENTIAL

Self-care also means setting boundaries and learning to say no when necessary. Taking on too much can lead to burnout, and this can have a negative impact on our ability to reach our potential. Learning to say no to things that don't align with our values and goals can free up time and energy to focus on the things that truly matter to us.

In conclusion, unlocking our inner potential is a journey that requires self-awareness, self-care, and the right mind-set. By setting clear, specific goals, focusing on our strengths, being proactive, building a supportive network, and being open to learning and growth. By being mindful and taking care of ourselves, and seeking feedback from others, we can tap into our inner potential and achieve the things we've always dreamed of. Remember, unlocking our inner potential is not a one-time event, it's a lifelong process. Keep an open mind, be patient with yourself and enjoy the journey.

02: The Power of Self-Discovery

The Power of Self-Discovery

Self-discovery is the process of uncovering one's true self, understanding one's strengths and weaknesses, and recognizing one's deepest desires and values. It is a journey of self-exploration that leads to personal growth and fulfillment. The power of self-discovery lies in its ability to empower individuals to take control of their lives and create the reality they desire.

The first step in the process of self-discovery is to look within oneself. This means examining one's thoughts, emotions, and behavior patterns. It is important to be honest with oneself and to acknowledge any negative thoughts or behaviors that may be holding one back. This can be difficult and uncomfortable, but it is essential for personal growth.

Once one has a better understanding of their thoughts and behaviors, the next step is to identify one's values and beliefs. Values are the principles that guide our actions and shape our worldview. They can include things like integrity, honesty, and compassion. Beliefs, on the other hand, are the assumptions and convictions we hold about ourselves and the world around us. It is important to be aware of our values and beliefs as they shape our actions and reactions to the world around us.

As one continues on their journey of self-discovery, it is important to set goals and create a plan of action. This means identifying the areas of one's life that they would like to improve, setting specific and measurable goals, and creating a plan of action to achieve those goals. This can include things like learning a new skill, starting a new hobby, or making changes to one's career.

One of the most powerful aspects of self-discovery is the ability to understand and accept one's true self. This means being comfortable with one's strengths and weaknesses and accepting oneself for who they are. It also means being open to change and growth, while still being true to oneself.

Self-discovery also involves recognizing and understanding one's deepest desires and passions. This means identifying what truly brings one joy and fulfillment, and making the conscious decision to pursue those things. This can be difficult, as it may involve taking risks and stepping outside of one's comfort zone, but it is essential for achieving true happiness and fulfillment.

Self-discovery also involves being mindful of one's relationships and interactions with others. This means being aware of how one's actions and words affect others and making conscious decisions to improve those interactions. It also means building strong and supportive relationships with others and learning to communicate effectively.

In conclusion, the power of self-discovery lies in its ability to empower individuals to take control of their lives and create the reality they desire. It involves looking within oneself, identifying one's values and beliefs, setting goals and creating a plan of action, understanding and accepting one's true self, recognizing one's deepest desires and passions, and being mindful of one's relationships and interactions with others. It is a journey that can lead to personal growth and fulfillment.

Self-discovery is a continuous process, and it is important to make time to reflect and evaluate one's progress regularly. Remember that self-discovery is not about perfection, it is about growth, and you will make mistakes, but that is okay, it is a part of the process. Keep an open mind, be patient with yourself, and don't be afraid to seek help or guidance if you need it. Remember that the power of self-discovery is within you and that you have the ability to create the life you desire.

Another important aspect of self-discovery is learning to let go of limiting beliefs and negative self-talk. These are the thoughts and beliefs that hold us back and prevent us from reaching our full potential. Examples of limiting beliefs include "I'm not good enough," "I'll never be successful," or "I can't do that." These beliefs can be deeply ingrained and can take time and effort to overcome.

One way to start changing limiting beliefs is to challenge them. Ask yourself where these beliefs came from and if they are truly accurate. It can also be helpful to reframe these beliefs in a more positive light. For example, instead of saying "I'm not good enough," try saying "I am constantly improving and working towards my goals."

It is also important to practice self-compassion during the process of self-discovery. This means being kind and understanding towards oneself, instead of being overly critical. Self-compassion involves recognizing that everyone makes mistakes and has flaws, and that it is normal to have negative thoughts and feelings. It also means treating oneself with the same kindness and understanding that one would offer to a friend.

Another important aspect of self-discovery is learning to take responsibility for one's actions and decisions. This means recognizing that one is in control of their own life and that they have the power to make changes. It also means being accountable for the consequences of one's actions and taking responsibility for the outcomes.

In addition to the above, Self-discovery also includes understanding and exploring one's cultural, ethnic, and social identity. This includes understanding one's own history and heritage and how that shapes one's perspective, values and beliefs. It also includes understanding the different cultural and social groups one belongs to and how those groups shape one's experiences and interactions with the world.

In conclusion, self-discovery is a continuous journey of personal growth and fulfillment. It involves looking within oneself, identifying one's values and beliefs, setting goals and creating a plan of action, understanding and accepting one's true self, recognizing one's deepest desires and passions, being mindful of one's relationships and interactions with others, let go of limiting beliefs and negative self-talk, practicing self-compassion and taking responsibility for one's actions, and understanding and exploring one's cultural, ethnic, and social identity. It is a powerful tool that can empower individuals to create the life they desire. Remember to be patient and kind to yourself, and don't be afraid to seek help and guidance when needed.

03: Setting and Achieving Goals

Setting and achieving goals is an essential part of personal and professional growth and development. Goals provide direction and motivation, helping us to focus our efforts and resources towards something specific and meaningful. But goal-setting is not always easy. In order to set and achieve goals that are truly meaningful and effective, it is important to understand the key principles and practices of goal-setting.

The first step in setting and achieving goals is to identify what you truly want. This may seem like an obvious step, but it is one that is often overlooked or rushed through. To identify what you truly want, you need to take the time to reflect on your values, passions, and aspirations. This will help you to identify what is truly important to you, and to set goals that are aligned with your values and passions.

Once you have identified what you truly want, the next step is to set specific, measurable, and achievable goals. Specific goals are those that are clear and specific, stating exactly what you want to achieve. Measurable goals are those that can be quantified and tracked, so that you can measure your progress and know when you have achieved your goal.

Achievable goals are those that are realistic and attainable, taking into account your current resources and circumstances.

In addition to setting specific, measurable, and achievable goals, it is also important to set goals that are time-bound. This means setting a deadline for when you want to achieve your goal. Having a deadline helps to create a sense of urgency and gives you a clear target to work towards. It also helps to keep you motivated and on track, as you can see the progress you are making towards your goal.

Once you have set your goals, the next step is to create a plan of action. This means breaking down your goals into smaller, manageable tasks and steps. This will help you to focus your efforts and resources, and to make steady progress towards your goal. It is also important to set milestones along the way, so that you can track your progress and adjust your plan as needed.

As you work towards your goals, it is important to stay motivated and focused. This can be challenging, especially when faced with obstacles or setbacks. One way to stay motivated is to remind yourself of why your goal is important to you, and to remind yourself of the benefits and rewards that you will gain by achieving your goal.

Another way to stay motivated is to surround yourself with positive and supportive people. This includes friends, family, and colleagues who will support and encourage you in your efforts to achieve your goals. It is also important to seek out mentors and role models who can provide guidance and inspiration.

Finally, it is important to celebrate your successes and to learn from your mistakes. When you achieve a goal, take the time to celebrate and acknowledge your accomplishment. This will help to boost your confidence and motivation, and will give you a sense of accomplishment and satisfaction. When you encounter obstacles or setbacks, take the time to reflect on what went wrong and to learn from your mistakes. This will help you to make adjustments and to improve your performance in the future.

In conclusion, setting and achieving goals is an essential part of personal and professional growth and development. It is important to identify what you truly want, to set specific, measurable, and achievable goals that are time-bound, to create a plan of action, to stay motivated and focused, to surround yourself with positive and supportive people, and to celebrate your successes and learn from your mistakes. By following these principles and practices, you can set and achieve goals that are truly meaningful and effective, and that will help you to achieve your full potential in life.

Another important aspect of goal setting is to be accountable for your actions. This means taking responsibility for your goals and being accountable for the steps you take to achieve them. This includes setting up a system for tracking your progress, such as a journal or spreadsheet, and regularly reviewing your progress to ensure you are on track. It also means being open to feedback and taking responsibility for any mistakes or setbacks you encounter along the way.

Another key aspect of goal setting is to be flexible and adaptable. This means being willing to change course or adjust your plans as needed. Sometimes, unforeseen circumstances or new information may arise that require you to change your approach. Being open to change and willing to adapt your plans will help you to stay on track and achieve your goals.

Additionally, it's important to have a positive attitude when working towards your goals. Having a positive mindset can help you to stay motivated, overcome obstacles, and believe in yourself. If you find yourself struggling to maintain a positive attitude, consider incorporating mindfulness practices like meditation or yoga into your daily routine.

Lastly, it's crucial to set goals that are challenging but not overwhelming. Setting goals that are too easy or unrealistic can lead to a lack of motivation and a lack of progress. On the other hand, setting goals that are too difficult can lead to frustration and burnout. It's important to find a balance that pushes you to grow and develop, but also allows you to maintain a healthy work-life balance.

In summary, setting and achieving goals is an essential part of personal and professional growth and development. It requires identifying what you truly want, setting specific, measurable, and achievable goals, creating a plan of action, staying motivated, surrounding yourself with positive and supportive people, celebrating your successes, learning from your mistakes, being accountable, being adaptable, having a positive attitude and setting challenging but not overwhelming goals. By following these principles and prac-

tices, you can set and achieve goals that are truly meaningful and effective, and that will help you to achieve your full
potential in life.

04: Overcoming Limiting Beliefs

Limiting beliefs are thoughts or ideas that we hold about ourselves that limit our potential and prevent us from reaching our goals. These beliefs can be deeply ingrained in our minds, and can be difficult to overcome. However, by understanding the nature of limiting beliefs and taking steps to challenge and replace them, we can break free from their hold and achieve greater success and fulfillment in our lives.

One of the first steps in overcoming limiting beliefs is to identify them. This can be difficult, as limiting beliefs are often subconscious and may not be immediately obvious. However, by paying attention to our thoughts and feelings, we can begin to notice patterns and themes that indicate the presence of limiting beliefs. For example, if we find ourselves consistently saying things like "I can't do that," "I'm not good enough," or "I'm not smart enough," these may be indicators of limiting beliefs.

Once we have identified our limiting beliefs, we can begin to challenge them. This can be done by asking ourselves questions such as: "Is this belief really true?" "Where did this belief come from?" "What evidence do I have to support this belief?" By questioning the validity of our limiting beliefs, we can begin to see them for what they are: self-imposed limitations that are not based on reality.

Another important step in overcoming limiting beliefs is to replace them with more empowering beliefs. This can be done by identifying the opposite of our limiting belief, and actively working to adopt that belief instead. For example, if our limiting belief is "I can't do that," we can replace it with the belief "I can do anything I set my mind to." By replacing our limiting beliefs with positive, empowering beliefs, we can shift our mindset and open ourselves up to new possibilities.

It's also important to remember that limiting beliefs are often based on past experiences, and that we are not defined by these experiences. We can learn from our past, but we do not have to be limited by it. We can choose to let go of past experiences and move forward, focusing on the present and the future.

In addition, it's helpful to surround ourselves with supportive people who believe in us and our abilities. This can be family, friends, or even a therapist or coach. Having people around us who believe in us and support us can help us to believe in ourselves and overcome our limiting beliefs.

It's also important to be kind to ourselves and practice self-compassion. Beating ourselves up and criticizing ourselves only reinforces limiting beliefs. Instead, we should try to be kind and understanding with ourselves, and acknowledge that we're all human and we all make mistakes.

Finally, practice visualization and affirmations. Visualizing ourselves achieving our goals and using affirmations can help us to overcome limiting beliefs by reinforcing positive thoughts and beliefs in our minds.

In conclusion, overcoming limiting beliefs is not easy, but it is possible. By identifying and challenging our limiting beliefs, replacing them with more empowering beliefs, and surrounding ourselves with supportive people, we can break free from the hold of limiting beliefs and achieve greater success and fulfillment in our lives. Remember to be kind to yourself, practice visualization, and affirmations.

Another powerful tool for overcoming limiting beliefs is mindfulness. Mindfulness is the practice of being present and fully engaged in the current moment, without judgment. When we are mindful, we can observe our thoughts and feelings without getting caught up in them. This allows us to gain perspective on our limiting beliefs and see them for what they are: just thoughts, not necessarily reality.

Mindfulness can be practiced through various techniques such as meditation, yoga, or simply taking a few deep breaths and focusing on the present moment. By incorporating mindfulness into our daily lives, we can learn to observe our thoughts and feelings without getting caught up in them, and gain a deeper understanding of the nature of our limiting beliefs.

Another effective strategy for overcoming limiting beliefs is to take action. Often, limiting beliefs stem from fear of failure or rejection. By taking small, manageable steps towards our goals, we can begin to challenge these fears and build confidence in our abilities. As we begin to see that we can accomplish what we set out to do, our limiting beliefs will lose their power over us.

It's also important to remember that change takes time and effort. Overcoming limiting beliefs is a process, and it's important to be patient and persistent. We may encounter setbacks along the way, but it's important to remember that these are just temporary and that with determination and perseverance, we can overcome any limiting belief and achieve our goals.

In conclusion, limiting beliefs can hold us back from reaching our full potential, but with the right tools and strategies, we can overcome them. By identifying our limiting beliefs, challenging them, replacing them with positive, empowering beliefs, practicing mindfulness, taking action, and being patient and persistent, we can break free from their hold and achieve greater success and fulfillment in our lives. Remember that change takes time and effort, but with determination and perseverance, anything is possible.

05: Mindset Mastery for Success

Mindset mastery is the key to achieving success in any area of life. It is the process of developing a positive and empowering mindset that allows you to overcome obstacles, set and achieve goals, and live a fulfilling life. In this chapter, we will explore the concept of mindset mastery and how you can use it to achieve success in your own life.

First, it is important to understand that mindset is the way that we think and perceive the world around us. Our mindset shapes our beliefs, attitudes, and behaviors, and ultimately determines our level of success in different areas of life. A positive and empowering mindset is essential for success, as it allows us to overcome obstacles, set and achieve goals, and live a fulfilling life.

One of the most important aspects of mindset mastery is the ability to control our thoughts. Our thoughts have a powerful impact on our emotions and behaviors, and we must learn to control them in order to achieve success. This means learning to identify and challenge negative thoughts, and replacing them with positive, empowering ones. It also means learning to focus on the present moment, rather than dwelling on the past or worrying about the future.

Another important aspect of mindset mastery is the ability to set and achieve goals. Setting and achieving goals is essential for success, as it allows us to move forward and make progress in our lives. However, it is important to set realistic and achievable goals, and to develop a plan for achieving them. This means breaking down larger goals into smaller, more manageable steps, and taking action towards achieving them on a regular basis.

In order to achieve success, it is also important to develop a growth mindset. A growth mindset is the belief that we can continue to grow and improve, regardless of our current circumstances. This means being open to new challenges, learning from our mistakes, and seeing failure as an opportunity to grow and learn. It also means being willing to take risks and try new things, even if there is a chance of failure.

In addition to developing a growth mindset, it is also important to develop a sense of self-awareness. Self-awareness is the ability to understand and accept our own strengths and weaknesses, and to use them to our advantage. This means taking the time to reflect on our own thoughts, emotions, and behaviors, and learning from them. It also means being honest with ourselves about our own limitations, and taking steps to overcome them.

Finally, it is important to develop a sense of resilience. Resilience is the ability to bounce back from setbacks and challenges, and to keep moving forward. This means learning to cope with difficult situations and to stay positive, even when things are not going well. It also means learning to take care of ourselves, both physically and mentally, in order to maintain our energy and motivation.

In conclusion, mindset mastery is the key to achieving success in any area of life. It is the process of developing a positive and empowering mindset that allows us to overcome obstacles, set and achieve goals, and live a fulfilling life. By learning to control our thoughts, set and achieve goals, develop a growth mindset, develop a sense of self-awareness, and develop a sense of resilience, we can master our mindsets and achieve success in all areas of our lives.

One practical way to apply the concepts of mindset mastery is through the use of affirmations. Affirmations are positive statements that we repeat to ourselves on a regular basis, in order to change our thoughts and beliefs. They can be used to challenge negative thoughts, reinforce positive beliefs, and set and achieve goals. For example, if you are struggling with self-doubt, you might use the affirmation "I am capable and worthy of success." If you are trying to overcome a fear, you might use the affirmation "I am courageous and strong." By repeating these affirmations on a regular basis, you can begin to change your thoughts and beliefs, and achieve a more positive and empowering mindset.

Another practical way to apply the concepts of mindset mastery is through visualization. Visualization is the process of creating a mental image of a desired outcome or goal. By visualizing the outcome that you want to achieve, you can create a more powerful and realistic image in your mind, which can help you to take the necessary steps to achieve that goal. For example, if you want to achieve a certain level of success in your career, you might visualize yourself in that role, and imagine the feelings and actions that would be necessary to achieve that level of success.

In addition, practicing mindfulness and meditation is a powerful tool for mastering your mindset. Mindfulness is the practice of being present and aware in the moment, without judgment. By practicing mindfulness, you can learn to be more aware of your thoughts and emotions, and to respond to them in a more constructive and positive way. Meditation is a powerful tool for reducing stress, increasing focus, and improving overall well-being. It can help you to develop a more positive and empowering mindset by increasing your awareness of your thoughts and emotions, and teaching you how to control them.

Finally, it is important to surround yourself with positive and supportive people. The people we surround ourselves with can have a powerful influence on our thoughts, emotions, and behaviors. By surrounding yourself with positive and supportive people, you can learn to think and act in a more positive and empowering way. This means seeking out the company of people who are positive, supportive, and encouraging, and limiting your exposure to people who are negative and critical.

In conclusion, mindset mastery is the key to achieving success in any area of life. By learning to control our thoughts, set and achieve goals, develop a growth mindset, develop a sense of self-awareness, and develop a sense of resilience, we can master our mindsets and achieve success in all areas of our lives. Practicing affirmations, visualization, mindfulness, meditation and surrounding yourself with positive people are powerful tools that can help us to achieve a positive and empowering mindset. Remember, success starts with a positive mindset, so take the time to master your mindset and enjoy the rewards of a successful life.

06: Personal Development for Growth

Personal development is the process of improving oneself in various areas of life, including emotional, physical, intellectual, and spiritual well-being. It involves setting goals, taking action, and making changes to improve one's overall quality of life. Personal development is an ongoing journey that requires commitment, self-awareness, and a willingness to learn and grow.

One of the key components of personal development is setting goals. Goals give direction and purpose to one's life, and provide a sense of accomplishment when achieved. It is important to set realistic and attainable goals that align with one's values and passions. It is also important to break down large goals into smaller, more manageable steps, and to track progress and celebrate successes along the way.

Another important aspect of personal development is self-awareness. This involves understanding one's thoughts, feelings, and behaviors, and how they affect one's life. Self-awareness allows individuals to identify areas where they need to improve and make necessary changes. It also enables them to be more mindful and present in the moment, and to make more conscious choices.

Personal development also requires taking action. This means being willing to step out of one's comfort zone, to try new things, and to take risks. It also means being open to learning and growth, and being willing to receive feedback and make necessary changes. It is important to remember that failure is a natural part of the learning process, and that it is through failure that we learn and grow.

In addition to the above, personal development also requires maintaining balance in one's life. This means taking care of one's physical and emotional well-being, and making time for self-care and relaxation. It also means maintaining healthy relationships, both with oneself and with others, and making time for leisure and hobbies.

Personal development is also about being of service to others. This means being kind and compassionate, and making a positive impact in the world. It also means being a role model and mentor to others, and sharing one's knowledge and experience to help others grow and develop.

In conclusion, personal development is a lifelong journey that requires commitment, self-awareness, and a willingness to learn and grow. It is about setting and achieving goals, taking action, maintaining balance, and being of service to others. It is a process that requires patience, perseverance, and a positive attitude, and it is through personal development that we can reach our full potential and live a fulfilling life.

Another important aspect of personal development is developing a growth mindset. A growth mindset is the belief that one's abilities and intelligence can be developed and improved through effort and learning. This mindset is in contrast to a fixed mindset, which is the belief that one's abilities and intelligence are set and cannot be changed.

Having a growth mindset is important for personal development because it allows individuals to embrace challenges and failures as opportunities for growth and learning. It also promotes resilience and perseverance in the face of adversity.

To develop a growth mindset, it is important to focus on the process of learning and growth, rather than the outcome. This means setting goals that are challenging but achievable, and being willing to put in the effort and work to achieve them. It also means being open to feedback, and using it as a tool for improvement.

Another way to develop a growth mindset is to surround oneself with people who have a growth mindset. This includes seeking out mentors and role models who embody the qualities of a growth mindset, and surrounding oneself with people who are supportive and encouraging of learning and growth.

In addition to all the above, personal development also involves developing emotional intelligence. Emotional intelligence is the ability to understand and manage one's own emotions, as well as the emotions of others. It is an important aspect of personal development because it allows individuals to communicate effectively, build and maintain relationships, and make better decisions.

To develop emotional intelligence, it is important to be aware of one's own emotions and how they affect one's thoughts and behaviors. It also means being able to identify and express emotions in a healthy way, and being able to empathize with and understand the emotions of others.

In conclusion, personal development is an ongoing journey

that requires commitment, self-awareness, and a willingness to learn and grow. It is about setting and achieving goals, taking action, maintaining balance, being of service to others, and developing a growth mindset and emotional intelligence. With the right mindset and approach, personal development can lead to a more fulfilling and satisfying life.

07: Building Resilience and Mental Toughness

Building resilience and mental toughness are essential skills for anyone looking to achieve success in life. These skills enable individuals to face challenges and adversity with determination, grit, and a positive attitude. In this chapter, we will explore the key concepts of resilience and mental toughness, as well as strategies for developing these skills.

Resilience is the ability to bounce back from difficult situations, to adapt to change, and to recover from setbacks. It is the capacity to maintain a positive outlook and to find meaning and purpose in adversity. Resilience is a key ingredient in mental toughness, which is the ability to perform at your best, even in the face of stress, pressure, and adversity.

There are several key strategies for building resilience and mental toughness. These include:

– Mindfulness: Mindfulness is the practice of being present in the moment and paying attention to your thoughts and emotions. It can help you to manage stress, improve focus, and build resilience.

07: BUILDING RESILIENCE AND MENTAL TOUGHNESS

– Positive Thinking: Focusing on positive thoughts and attitudes can help to build resilience and mental toughness. It is important to surround yourself with positive people and to think positively about yourself and your abilities.

– Exercise: Regular exercise has been shown to improve mood, reduce stress, and boost resilience. Engage in physical activities that you enjoy, such as running, cycling, or swimming.

– Sleep: Getting a good night's sleep is essential for maintaining good mental health and building resilience. Aim for 7-9 hours of sleep each night.

– Support Network: Building a strong support network of family and friends can help to provide emotional support and a sense of belonging. Surround yourself with people who will encourage and support you.

– Set goals: Setting goals gives you a sense of direction and purpose. It can help you to focus on what you want to achieve and to work towards it. Set both short-term and long-term goals and make a plan to achieve them.

– Learn from failure: Failure is a part of life, and it is important to learn from it. When things don't go as planned, use it as an opportunity to learn and grow. Failure can be a valuable teacher and can help you to build resilience and mental toughness.

– Practice Gratitude: Practicing gratitude can help to shift your focus from negative thoughts and emotions to positive ones. It can also help you to appreciate what you have and to develop a sense of contentment.

–Seek professional help: If you are struggling with mental health issues or are feeling overwhelmed, seek professional help. A therapist or counselor can help you to work through your feelings and to develop strategies for building resilience and mental toughness.

In conclusion, building resilience and mental toughness is essential for achieving success in life. It enables individuals to face challenges and adversity with determination, grit, and a positive attitude. By incorporating mindfulness, positive thinking, exercise, sleep, a support network, setting goals, learning from failure, practicing gratitude and seeking professional help, you can develop these skills and become more resilient and mentally tough.

Another important aspect of building resilience and mental toughness is learning to manage stress. Stress is a natural part of life, but when it becomes chronic, it can have a negative impact on our physical and mental health. Chronic stress can lead to conditions such as depression, anxiety, and heart disease.

One way to manage stress is through stress-reduction techniques such as deep breathing, progressive muscle relaxation, and meditation. These techniques can help to calm the mind and relax the body, making it easier to handle stress.

Another way to manage stress is through time management. Being able to effectively manage your time can help you to prioritize tasks, avoid procrastination, and reduce feelings of overwhelm. This can help to reduce stress and improve your overall well-being.

It is also important to maintain a healthy lifestyle. Eating a balanced diet, getting regular exercise, and getting enough sleep are all important for maintaining good physical and mental health. These activities can help to reduce stress and improve overall well-being.

Another important aspect of building resilience and mental

toughness is learning to develop a growth mindset. People with a growth mindset believe that their abilities can be developed through effort and learning. They view challenges and failures as opportunities for growth and learning. On the other hand, people with a fixed mindset believe that their abilities are fixed and cannot be changed. They tend to avoid challenges and give up easily when faced with difficulty.

Adopting a growth mindset can help you to become more resilient and mentally tough. It can help you to view challenges and setbacks as opportunities for growth and learning, rather than as personal failures. This can help you to develop a more positive attitude and to become more resilient in the face of adversity.

Finally, it is important to remember that building resilience and mental toughness takes time and effort. It is not something that can be achieved overnight. It is a lifelong process that requires patience, perseverance, and a willingness to learn and grow. With the right mindset and strategies, anyone can develop these important skills and become more resilient and mentally tough.

07: BUILDING RESILIENCE AND MENTAL TOUGHNESS

In conclusion, building resilience and mental toughness is a lifelong process that requires patience, perseverance and the right mindset. By incorporating mindfulness, positive thinking, exercise, sleep, a support network, setting goals, learning from failure, practicing gratitude, seeking professional help, managing stress, maintaining a healthy lifestyle, developing a growth mindset and time management, you can develop these skills and become more resilient and mentally tough. This will help you to face challenges and adversity with determination, grit, and a positive attitude, and to achieve your goals and aspirations in life.

08: Embracing Failure and Learning from Mistakes

Embracing failure and learning from mistakes is an essential part of personal and professional growth. The ability to recognize and learn from failure is a key component of success, as it enables individuals and organizations to identify and correct their weaknesses, leading to improved performance and increased effectiveness.

One of the most important things to understand about failure is that it is a natural and inevitable part of life. No one is immune to failure, and everyone makes mistakes. This is especially true when it comes to learning and trying new things. The key to success is not avoiding failure, but rather embracing it and using it as a learning opportunity.

When we fail, it is important to take a step back and assess what went wrong. This process of reflection and analysis can help us to identify the specific mistakes that were made, as well as the underlying causes of those mistakes. By understanding the root causes of our failures, we can take steps to prevent them from happening again in the future.

It is also important to remember that failure is not always a bad thing. In fact, many of the most successful people in history have failed multiple times before achieving success. Thomas Edison, for example, is said to have failed over 1000 times before finally inventing the light bulb. He famously said "I have not failed. I've just found 10,000 ways that won't work." Failure can be a source of valuable information and can help us to learn and grow in ways that success alone cannot.

Another key aspect of embracing failure and learning from mistakes is developing a growth mindset. A growth mindset is the belief that one's abilities and intelligence can be developed through effort and learning. This mindset is in contrast to a fixed mindset, which holds that one's abilities and intelligence are fixed and cannot be changed. Those with a growth mindset view failure as an opportunity to learn and grow, while those with a fixed mindset tend to view failure as a personal failure and give up easily.

In order to develop a growth mindset, it is important to focus on the process of learning and improvement, rather than the outcome. Instead of fixating on the end result, focus on the steps you are taking to achieve it. This will help you to stay motivated and resilient in the face of failure.

It is also important to develop a sense of self-compassion. Be kind to yourself when you make mistakes and remember that everyone fails. Don't beat yourself up over your failures and instead focus on the lessons you can learn from them.

In addition, it is important to surround yourself with supportive people who will encourage and support you in your efforts to learn from your mistakes. Having a supportive network can help you to stay motivated and on track, even when things get tough.

In conclusion, embracing failure and learning from mistakes is an essential part of personal and professional growth. Failure is a natural and inevitable part of life and should be viewed as an opportunity to learn and grow. By understanding the root causes of our failures, developing a growth mindset, and surrounding ourselves with supportive people, we can learn from our mistakes and achieve greater success in the long run.

Another important aspect of embracing failure and learning from mistakes is the ability to take action and make meaningful changes. Simply recognizing and analyzing your failures is not enough; you must also take concrete steps to address the issues that led to those failures. This could involve making changes to your habits, processes, or systems, or seeking out additional training or resources to help you improve.

One way to take action and make meaningful changes is to set specific, measurable goals for yourself. Setting clear, measurable goals will give you a sense of direction and purpose, and will help you to stay focused and motivated as you work to overcome your failures. Additionally, tracking your progress and measuring your results will help you to see the impact of your efforts and make any necessary adjustments.

Another important aspect is to be open to feedback and willing to listen to others. Feedback is a valuable tool for learning and growth, and it can help you to identify areas where you need to improve. Be open to constructive criticism and take it as an opportunity to learn and grow. Additionally, seek out feedback from a diverse group of people, including mentors, peers, and subordinates.

It's also important to learn to accept responsibility for your mistakes and not to blame others or external factors. Blaming others or external factors for your failures will only serve to hold you back from learning and growing. Instead, take ownership of your mistakes and use them as an opportunity to learn and improve.

Finally, it's essential to be patient with yourself. Changing habits and learning new skills takes time, and progress will not always be linear. Be patient with yourself and give yourself time to learn and grow. Remember that failure is a natural part of the learning process and it's not the end of the journey.

In summary, embracing failure and learning from mistakes is an essential part of personal and professional growth. It's important to understand that failure is a natural and inevitable part of life and to view it as an opportunity to learn and grow. Develop a growth mindset, surround yourself with supportive people, take action and make meaningful changes, be open to feedback, accept responsibility, and be patient with yourself. By doing these things, you will be able to learn from your mistakes and achieve greater success in the long run.

09: Time Management and Productivity

Time management and productivity are essential skills for achieving success in both personal and professional settings. By managing your time effectively, you can accomplish more in less time, reduce stress, and improve overall satisfaction with your life.

The first step in effective time management is setting clear goals. Without goals, it is difficult to know what to prioritize and how to allocate your time. Setting specific, measurable, achievable, relevant, and time-bound (SMART) goals can help you stay focused and motivated.

Next, it is important to create a schedule or to-do list. This can be done using a variety of tools such as a calendar, a planner, or a productivity app. Make sure to include all of your daily tasks, as well as any upcoming deadlines or appointments. Prioritize your tasks based on their importance and urgency.

One effective technique for managing your time is the Pomodoro Technique. This method involves breaking your work into 25-minute intervals, called "Pomodoros," with short breaks in between. After four Pomodoros, take a longer break to rest and recharge. This technique helps to increase focus and prevent burnout.

Another key aspect of time management is learning to say "no." Many people struggle with overcommitment, leading to feelings of overwhelm and stress. By being selective about what you take on, you can focus on the most important tasks and avoid unnecessary distractions.

Additionally, it is important to minimize interruptions and distractions. This can be done by turning off notifications on your phone, closing unnecessary tabs on your computer, and working in a quiet, distraction-free environment.

One of the most effective ways to boost productivity is to stay organized. Having a clean and organized workspace can help you stay focused and reduce stress. Additionally, taking the time to declutter and organize your digital life can help you be more productive.

Another way to boost productivity is to take regular breaks. Taking short breaks throughout the day can help improve focus and creativity, and prevent burnout.

Finally, it is important to practice self-care and maintain a healthy work-life balance. This can include things like getting enough sleep, eating well, and engaging in regular physical activity. Additionally, make sure to set aside time for leisure and relaxation to avoid burnout.

In conclusion, time management and productivity are essential skills for achieving success in both personal and professional settings. By setting clear goals, creating a schedule, using effective techniques, minimizing interruptions and distractions, staying organized, taking regular breaks, and practicing self-care, you can improve your productivity and achieve a better work-life balance.

Another key aspect of time management is delegation. Many people try to do everything themselves, leading to feelings of burnout and a lack of productivity. By delegating tasks to others, you can focus on the most important tasks and achieve more in less time.

When delegating tasks, it is important to choose the right person for the job. Consider the skills and experience of the person you are delegating to, and make sure they have the necessary resources and support to complete the task successfully.

It is also important to provide clear instructions and expectations when delegating tasks. This will help ensure that the task is completed correctly and on time.

Another way to boost productivity is through the use of technology. There are many productivity apps and tools available that can help you stay organized, manage your schedule, and track your progress.

One popular app is Trello, which allows you to create boards and cards for different tasks and projects. This can help you stay organized and on top of your to-do list.

Another app is RescueTime, which tracks your activity on your device and provides reports on how you spend your time. This can help you identify areas where you might be wasting time and make adjustments to your schedule.

Finally, it is important to remember that time management and productivity are ongoing processes. You will encounter obstacles and setbacks along the way, but by remaining focused and committed to your goals, you can continue to improve your productivity and achieve your desired results.

In conclusion, time management and productivity are essential skills that can help you achieve success in both personal and professional settings. By setting clear goals, creating a schedule, using effective techniques, minimizing interruptions and distractions, staying organized, taking regular breaks, practicing self-care, delegating tasks, and utilizing technology, you can improve your productivity and achieve a better work-life balance. Remember that time management and productivity are ongoing process and will require consistent effort and focus to maintain.

10: Building Strong Relationships

Building strong relationships is a key aspect of human life. Whether it is a romantic relationship, a friendship, or a professional partnership, having a network of supportive and trustworthy people is essential for our well-being and happiness. However, building strong relationships can be challenging, as it requires effort, communication, and a willingness to be vulnerable. In this chapter, we will explore some of the key elements of building strong relationships and discuss strategies for maintaining and strengthening them.

One of the most important elements of building strong relationships is effective communication. Communication is the foundation upon which all relationships are built, and it is essential for understanding and connecting with others. When communicating with others, it is important to be clear and direct, to listen actively, and to express ourselves honestly and authentically. Additionally, it is essential to be aware of nonverbal cues and to pay attention to how our words and actions are being received.

Another key element of building strong relationships is trust. Trust is the foundation of any healthy relationship and is built over time through consistency, honesty, and reliability. Trust is also built through vulnerability, which allows us to open up and share our thoughts, feelings, and experiences with others. When we are vulnerable, we are able to build deeper connections with others and create a sense of intimacy.

Empathy is also crucial for building strong relationships. Empathy is the ability to understand and share the feelings of others, and it is essential for building trust and understanding. When we are able to put ourselves in the shoes of others and understand their perspective, we are better able to communicate and connect with them. Additionally, empathy helps us to be more compassionate and understanding, which can lead to deeper and more meaningful relationships.

Another key element of building strong relationships is shared values and goals. When we share similar values and goals with others, we are more likely to connect with them and form a deeper bond. Additionally, shared values and goals provide a sense of purpose and direction, which can help to strengthen relationships over time.

Finally, building strong relationships also requires a willingness to compromise and to work through conflicts. Conflict is a natural part of any relationship, and it is essential to learn how to handle it in a healthy and constructive way. This requires effective communication, empathy, and a willingness to see things from the other person's perspective. Additionally, it is important to be willing to compromise and to work together to find a solution that is acceptable to both parties.

In conclusion, building strong relationships is an essential aspect of human life and requires effort, communication, and a willingness to be vulnerable. To build strong relationships, it is important to communicate effectively, build trust, practice empathy, share values and goals, and be willing to compromise and work through conflicts. By implementing these strategies, we can create deep and meaningful connections with others and improve our overall well-being and happiness.

Another important aspect of building strong relationships is being reliable and dependable. When we make commitments, it is important to follow through on them and to be there for the people we care about. Being dependable builds trust and shows that we are committed to the relationship.

It's also important to be flexible and open to change. Relationships can change over time, and it's important to be willing to adapt and evolve as needed. This can include learning new things about each other, trying new activities, or even changing the nature of the relationship. Being open to change allows us to grow together and deepen our connection.

Additionally, it is important to show appreciation and gratitude towards the people in our lives. Expressing gratitude and appreciation helps to build positive feelings and can strengthen the bond in a relationship. A simple thank you or a thoughtful gesture can go a long way in showing someone that we appreciate them.

It's also important to set boundaries and respect the boundaries of others. In any relationship, it's important to have a clear understanding of what is and isn't acceptable behavior. Setting boundaries allows us to maintain our sense of self and ensures that we are treated with respect. Additionally, when we respect the boundaries of others, we are showing them that we care about their well-being and are committed to the relationship.

In addition to all the above, it is also important to always be open to learning and growing. This means being open to feedback, taking the time to reflect on our actions and behavior, and being willing to make changes when necessary. Additionally, it means being open to learning about others and their perspectives, which can help us to build deeper connections and understanding.

Finally, building strong relationships also require patience and consistency. As with anything worthwhile, building and maintaining strong relationships takes time and effort. It requires patience to work through challenges and consistency in our actions and behavior. It's important to remember that relationships are not always easy, but with patience and consistency, they can be incredibly rewarding.

In conclusion, building strong relationships is a complex and multi-faceted process that requires effort, communication, trust, empathy, shared values, goals and the willingness to work through conflicts, be reliable and dependable, be flexible and open to change, show appreciation and gratitude, set boundaries and respect the boundaries of others, be open to learning and growing, and patience and consistency. By understanding and implementing these strategies, we can create deep, meaningful and long-lasting relation-ships that will enrich our lives and bring us happiness and fulfillment.

11: The Importance of Self-Care

Self-care is the practice of taking care of one's own physical, mental, and emotional well-being. It is an essential part of maintaining good health and overall well-being, and it is something that should be prioritized by everyone.

One of the main reasons why self-care is so important is that it helps us to manage stress. Stress is a normal part of life, but it can become overwhelming if it is not managed properly. When we practice self-care, we are taking steps to reduce stress and improve our overall well-being. This can include things like exercise, relaxation techniques, and healthy eating.

Another important aspect of self-care is that it helps us to be more present in our lives. When we are constantly busy and stressed, it can be difficult to focus on the present moment and enjoy the things that are happening around us. By taking care of ourselves, we can be more present and enjoy life more fully.

Self-care also helps us to be more resilient. When we are feeling stressed and overwhelmed, it can be difficult to bounce back from setbacks and challenges. By taking care of ourselves, we are building our resilience and our ability to cope with difficult situations.

One of the most important things to remember about self-care is that it is not a one-time thing. It is a ongoing process that requires consistent effort and attention. This can include setting aside time each day for self-care activities, such as exercise or meditation, as well as making sure to get enough sleep and eat a healthy diet.

It is also important to remember that self-care is not selfish. Taking care of ourselves is not only important for our own well-being, but it also allows us to be better equipped to help and support others.

One way to practice self-care is by setting boundaries. This means learning to say no to things that don't serve us, and prioritizing our own needs. This can be difficult for some people, as they may feel guilty or selfish for putting themselves first. However, setting boundaries is a vital part of self-care and can help us to avoid burnout and maintain a healthy balance in our lives.

Another way to practice self-care is by practicing mindfulness. This means being present in the moment and paying attention to our thoughts and feelings. This can help us to identify and address any negative thoughts or emotions that may be impacting our well-being.

Other self-care practices include exercise, journaling, reading, getting enough sleep, spending time in nature and socializing with loved ones.

In conclusion, self-care is an essential part of maintaining good health and overall well-being. It helps us to manage stress, be more present in our lives, be more resilient, and set boundaries. It is an ongoing process that requires consistent effort and attention. By making self-care a priority, we can improve our overall well-being and enjoy life more fully.

Another important aspect of self-care is self-compassion. Self-compassion involves treating ourselves with kindness and understanding, rather than judgment and criticism. It involves recognizing that we all have flaws and make mistakes, and that this is a normal part of being human.

When we practice self-compassion, we are more likely to be resilient in the face of challenges, and less likely to be overwhelmed by negative emotions. We are also more likely to set realistic goals for ourselves, and to treat ourselves kindly when we fall short of these goals.

Self-compassion can be practiced in a variety of ways. One way is through self-compassionate self-talk, which involves speaking to ourselves in a kind and understanding way. This can involve reframing negative thoughts and emotions, and reminding ourselves that we are not alone in our struggles.

Another way to practice self-compassion is through mindfulness. This means being present in the moment and paying attention to our thoughts and feelings without judgment. Mindfulness can help us to be more compassionate towards ourselves, as we learn to accept ourselves as we are, rather than constantly striving for perfection.

Self-compassion can also be practiced through self-care activities such as exercise, journaling, and spending time in nature. These activities can help us to feel more relaxed and centered, which can in turn help us to be more compassionate towards ourselves.

In addition to self-compassion, self-care also includes self-awareness and self-exploration. This means taking the time to understand our own thoughts, feelings, and behaviors, and to explore what is truly important to us. By gaining a deeper understanding of ourselves, we can make more informed decisions about how to take care of ourselves and live a fulfilling life.

Self-care is also important for our relationships. When we take care of ourselves, we are better equipped to be there for others and to build healthy and meaningful relationships. When we neglect our own well-being, we may find ourselves feeling resentful and disconnected from others.

In conclusion, self-care is a vital component of overall well-being and is essential for managing stress, being present, being resilient, setting boundaries, practicing self-compassion and self-awareness, and fostering healthy relationships. It is not a luxury, but a necessity. It is important to make self-care a priority, and to find ways to incorporate it into our daily lives. By doing so, we can enjoy a more fulfilling and meaningful life.

12: Unlocking Your Creativity and Innovation

Unlocking Your Creativity and Innovation

Creativity and innovation are essential for personal and professional growth, as well as for the advancement of society. They are the driving forces behind new ideas, products, and solutions. However, many people feel that they are not creative or innovative and struggle to generate new ideas. The good news is that creativity and innovation are skills that can be developed and nurtured. In this chapter, we will explore ways to unlock your creativity and innovation and bring new ideas to life.

First, it is important to understand that creativity and innovation are not the same thing. Creativity refers to the ability to generate new ideas, while innovation refers to the ability to put those ideas into action. Creativity is the spark, and innovation is the fire. Both are important for creating new and valuable things.

One key to unlocking your creativity is to be open to new experiences and perspectives. This means exposing yourself to diverse people, cultures, and ideas. It also means being willing to take risks and try new things, even if they seem strange or uncomfortable at first. This kind of open-mindedness can help you see the world in new ways and generate new ideas.

Another key to unlocking your creativity is to be curious. Curiosity is the desire to learn and understand more about the world around you. It is the drive to ask questions and seek answers. Being curious means being open to new information and being willing to explore new areas of knowledge. This kind of curiosity can help you see connections and patterns that others might miss, which can lead to new ideas.

Another way to unlock your creativity and innovation is to be willing to play and experiment. Play is a powerful tool for generating new ideas. It allows you to relax, let go of your preconceptions, and explore new possibilities. Experimenting allows you to test different ideas and see what works and what doesn't. This kind of experimentation and play can help you find new solutions to problems and create new products.

Another way to boost creativity and innovation is to collaborate with others. Collaboration allows you to share ideas and perspectives, which can lead to new and better ideas. It also allows you to combine different skills and talents to create something new. Collaboration can also increase accountability and motivation, which can help you stay focused and committed to your ideas.

To unleash your innovation, you need to be willing to take action. Innovation is not just about having good ideas, but also about putting those ideas into action. This means taking risks, making mistakes, and learning from them. It also means being willing to fail. Failure is a natural part of the innovation process and can provide valuable lessons and insights.

In addition to these general tips, there are specific techniques that can help you boost your creativity and innovation. One such technique is brainstorming. Brainstorming is a process of generating new ideas by free-associating and building on the ideas of others. To brainstorm effectively, it is important to set aside judgment, encourage wild ideas, and build on the ideas of others.

Another technique is lateral thinking. Lateral thinking is a process of solving problems by looking at them from different perspectives. This can involve looking at a problem from a different angle, using a different frame of reference, or using a different set of assumptions. Lateral thinking can help you generate new ideas and find new solutions to problems.

Finally, it is important to note that unlocking your creativity and innovation is not a one-time event but a continuous process. It requires regular practice, experimentation, and reflection. It also requires a willingness to change and adapt. By being open-minded, curious, playful, collaborative, and willing to take action, you can unlock your creativity and innovation and bring new ideas to life.

One way to continue the process of unlocking your creativity and innovation is to set aside dedicated time for brainstorming and idea generation. This can be done individually or as part of a group. It is also important to make space for experimentation and play in your daily routine. This can be done by setting aside time for hobbies or taking on new projects outside of your usual work.

Another way to continue the process is to seek feedback and input from others. This can be done by sharing your ideas with trusted colleagues or friends and asking for their thoughts and suggestions. It is also important to be open to constructive criticism and use it as a learning opportunity.

Finally, it is important to stay informed about the latest trends and developments in your field. This can be done by reading industry publications, attending conferences, and networking with other professionals. By staying up-to-date, you can gain new perspectives and insights that can lead to new ideas.

In conclusion, creativity and innovation are essential skills that can be developed and nurtured. By being open-minded, curious, playful, collaborative, and willing to take action, you can unlock your creativity and innovation and bring new ideas to life. It is important to set aside dedicated time for brainstorming and idea generation, seek feedback and input from others, and stay informed about the latest trends and developments in your field. By continuously working on your creativity and innovation, you can create new and valuable things, both for yourself and for the world.

13: Overcoming Fear and Anxiety

Fear and anxiety are natural human emotions that everyone experiences at some point in their lives. They are a response to perceived threats and can be helpful in certain situations, such as preparing for a job interview or keeping us safe from danger. However, when fear and anxiety become overwhelming and start to interfere with our daily lives, they can become a problem. This chapter will explore the causes of fear and anxiety, the differences between the two, and strategies for overcoming them.

Causes of Fear and Anxiety

Fear and anxiety are triggered by different situations and can be caused by a variety of factors. Some common causes include:

– Trauma or past experiences: Trauma, such as physical or emotional abuse, can cause long-term fear and anxiety.

– Genetics: Some people may be more prone to anxiety due to genetic factors.

– Brain chemistry: Imbalances in brain chemicals, such as serotonin and dopamine, can contribute to anxiety.

– Medical conditions: Certain medical conditions, such as heart disease or thyroid problems, can cause anxiety.

– Environmental factors: Stressful life events, such as a job loss or a move to a new place, can trigger fear and anxiety.

Differences between Fear and Anxiety

While fear and anxiety are closely related, they are not the same thing. Fear is a natural response to a specific, immediate threat. For example, if you see a snake in your path while hiking, you will feel fear. It's a natural response that prepares you to either fight or flee. Anxiety, on the other hand, is a general feeling of unease that can be caused by a wide range of things. It's a response to potential future threats, such as worrying about a job interview or a medical test.

Overcoming Fear and Anxiety

There are several strategies that can help you overcome fear and anxiety. These include:

– Cognitive-behavioral therapy (CBT): This type of therapy focuses on identifying and changing negative thoughts and behaviors that contribute to fear and anxiety.

– Exposure therapy: This type of therapy involves gradually exposing yourself to the thing that you fear in a controlled environment. This can help you learn that the feared thing is not as dangerous as you thought.

– Medication: Antidepressant and anti-anxiety medications can be effective in reducing fear and anxiety.

– Relaxation techniques: Relaxation techniques, such as deep breathing, yoga, and meditation, can help reduce stress and anxiety.

– Self-care: Taking care of yourself by getting enough sleep, eating well, and engaging in physical activity can help reduce anxiety and promote overall well-being.

Conclusion

Fear and anxiety are natural human emotions that can become a problem when they become overwhelming. Understanding the causes and differences between the two can help you develop strategies for overcoming them. Some effective strategies include cognitive-behavioral therapy, exposure therapy, medication, relaxation techniques and self-care. Remember, it is important to seek professional help if your fear or anxiety is interfering with your daily life. With the right strategies and support, it is possible to overcome fear and anxiety and lead a fulfilling life.

It's also important to note that overcoming fear and anxiety is not a one-time process, but rather a continuous journey. It's important to be patient with yourself and to not expect to be completely free from fear and anxiety overnight. Additionally, it's important to acknowledge that setbacks can happen, and that's okay. The important thing is to keep moving forward and to not let setbacks discourage you from continuing to work on overcoming your fears and anxieties.

Another strategy that can be helpful in overcoming fear and anxiety is mindfulness. Mindfulness is the practice of being present and fully engaged in the current moment, without judgment. Mindfulness can help reduce anxiety by helping you focus on the present rather than dwelling on the past or worrying about the future. Mindfulness practices such as meditation, yoga, or tai chi can help you develop mindfulness skills.

Another effective strategy is to practice self-compassion. Self-compassion involves treating yourself with the same kindness and understanding that you would offer to a friend. It also includes acknowledging that everyone makes mistakes and has difficult times, and that it's normal to struggle. When you're feeling anxious, try to remind yourself that it's normal to feel this way and that you're not alone.

Lastly, it's important to build a support system. Support from friends and family can be a powerful tool in overcoming fear and anxiety. Talking to someone you trust about your fears and anxieties can help you gain a different perspective and feel less alone. Joining a support group can also be helpful as it allows you to connect with others who are going through similar experiences.

In conclusion, fear and anxiety are natural human emotions that can become overwhelming. However, with the right strategies, support and patience, it's possible to overcome them and lead a fulfilling life. Remember to take it one step at a time, be patient with yourself and to seek professional help if needed.

14: Building Confidence and Self-Esteem

Building confidence and self-esteem is a vital aspect of personal development and can greatly impact an individual's ability to navigate through life's challenges. Confidence is the belief in one's own abilities, qualities, and judgments, while self-esteem is the overall sense of self-worth and value. Both are closely related and often work together to affect an individual's overall well-being.

There are several key strategies that can be used to build confidence and self-esteem. One of the most important is to set and achieve goals. Setting small, manageable goals for oneself can help to build confidence as one becomes more successful in achieving them. It is also important to have a positive attitude and to focus on the present moment, rather than dwelling on past failures or worrying about future challenges.

Another important strategy is to practice self-care and to engage in activities that promote physical and emotional well-being. This can include regular exercise, eating a healthy diet, getting enough sleep, and taking time to relax and de-stress. Additionally, surrounding oneself with positive and supportive people can also help to build confidence and self-esteem.

It's also important to practice self-compassion and self-acceptance, which means treating oneself with kindness and understanding, rather than harshly judging oneself for mistakes or perceived shortcomings. This means being kind and forgiving towards oneself, and to take a more positive and understanding perspective of oneself.

Another effective way to build confidence and self-esteem is to challenge negative thoughts and beliefs. Negative thoughts and beliefs can be limiting, and can prevent an individual from reaching their full potential. By recognizing and challenging negative thoughts, one can begin to replace them with more positive and empowering thoughts.

It's also important to be mindful of one's self-talk and to be aware of the language and phrases we use to describe ourselves and our abilities. Instead of using negative or self-deprecating language, it's important to use positive and empowering language to describe oneself.

Lastly, it's important to remember that building confidence and self-esteem is a continuous process that takes time and effort. It's important to be patient and compassionate with oneself and to remember that setbacks and failures are a normal part of the process. It's also important to remember that there is no "perfect" level of confidence or self-esteem and that everyone's journey is unique.

In conclusion, building confidence and self-esteem is an important aspect of personal development that can greatly impact an individual's ability to navigate through life's challenges. By setting and achieving goals, practicing self-care, surrounding oneself with positive and supportive people, practicing self-compassion and self-acceptance, challenging negative thoughts and beliefs, being mindful of one's self-talk, and being patient and compassionate with oneself, one can begin to build and maintain confidence and self-esteem. Remember, it's a continuous journey and it's important to be kind and compassionate with oneself through the process.

Another important aspect of building confidence and self-esteem is learning to embrace and accept one's uniqueness. Everyone is different and has their own unique set of strengths, weaknesses, and experiences. It is important to focus on and appreciate one's own individuality, rather than constantly comparing oneself to others or trying to conform to societal norms. Embracing one's uniqueness can help to build self-acceptance and self-confidence.

Another important tool for building confidence and self-esteem is positive affirmations. Positive affirmations are statements that are repeated to oneself with the intention of promoting a positive mindset and attitude. Examples of positive affirmations include "I am worthy", "I am capable", "I am strong", "I am in control of my thoughts and emotions". Repeating these affirmations to oneself on a daily basis can help to change negative thought patterns and promote a more positive and confident mindset.

It is also important to learn how to handle criticism and constructive feedback in a healthy way. Criticism and feedback can be difficult to hear, but they can also be valuable tools for growth and improvement. Instead of taking criticism and feedback personally, it is important to approach them objectively and use them as opportunities to learn and improve.

In addition to these strategies, it can also be helpful to seek professional support such as therapy or counseling. A therapist or counselor can help to identify and work through underlying issues that may be contributing to low confidence and self-esteem. They can also provide additional strategies and tools for building confidence and self-esteem.

Lastly, it's important to remember that building confidence and self-esteem is a continuous process that takes time and effort. It's important to be patient and compassionate with oneself and to remember that setbacks and failures are a normal part of the process. It's also important to remember that there is no "perfect" level of confidence or self-esteem and that everyone's journey is unique.

In conclusion, building confidence and self-esteem is an important aspect of personal development that can greatly impact an individual's ability to navigate through life's challenges. By setting and achieving goals, practicing self-care, surrounding oneself with positive and supportive people, practicing self-compassion and self-acceptance, challenging negative thoughts and beliefs, being mindful of one's self-talk, and being patient and compassionate with oneself, embracing one's uniqueness, using positive affirmations, handling criticism and feedback in a healthy way, and seeking professional support can all be effective ways to build and maintain confidence and self-esteem. Remember, it's a continuous journey and it's important to be kind and compassionate with oneself through the process.

15: Harnessing the Power of Positive Thinking

The power of positive thinking is a powerful tool that can help individuals achieve their goals and lead happier, more fulfilling lives. Positive thinking is the practice of focusing on the good in any situation and maintaining a positive outlook, even in the face of adversity. By harnessing the power of positive thinking, individuals can overcome challenges, improve their mental and physical health, and achieve greater success in their personal and professional lives.

One of the key benefits of positive thinking is that it can help individuals to overcome obstacles and achieve their goals. When faced with a difficult task or challenge, those who maintain a positive outlook are more likely to find solutions and persist in the face of adversity. This is because positive thinking allows individuals to see the best in any situation, even when things are not going well. By focusing on the good, individuals can find the motivation and inspiration they need to continue working towards their goals, even when things get tough.

Another important benefit of positive thinking is that it can improve mental and physical health. Positive thinking is associated with lower levels of stress and anxiety, and has been shown to boost the immune system, decrease the risk of heart disease, and reduce symptoms of depression and other mental health conditions. This is because positive thinking helps individuals to focus on the present moment and find the good in any situation, rather than dwelling on the past or worrying about the future.

In addition to these benefits, positive thinking can also lead to greater success in both personal and professional life. Positive thinking can help individuals to build stronger relationships, become more successful in their careers, and achieve greater financial success. This is because individuals who maintain a positive outlook are more likely to be confident, optimistic, and motivated, which are all traits that are highly valued by employers and others in the professional world.

One of the most effective ways to harness the power of positive thinking is to practice daily affirmations. Affirmations are positive statements that individuals can repeat to themselves on a regular basis to help them focus on the good in any situation. For example, an affirmation might be "I am strong and capable of achieving my goals" or "I am surrounded by love and support." By repeating these affirmations on a daily basis, individuals can train their minds to focus on the positive, which can help them to overcome challenges and achieve greater success.

Another effective way to harness the power of positive thinking is to practice gratitude. Gratitude is the practice of focusing on the things in one's life that one is thankful for, rather than dwelling on the things that are missing. By taking time each day to reflect on the things that one is grateful for, individuals can shift their focus from negative thoughts to positive ones, which can help them to maintain a more positive outlook.

Finally, it is important to surround oneself with positive people. Surrounding oneself with positive people can help to create a supportive environment that encourages positive thinking. Being around positive people can help to reduce stress, improve mental and physical health, and provide support and encouragement when things get tough.

In conclusion, the power of positive thinking is a powerful tool that can help individuals to achieve their goals, improve their mental and physical health, and lead happier, more fulfilling lives. By harnessing the power of positive thinking through techniques such as affirmations, gratitude, and surrounding oneself with positive people, individuals can overcome challenges and achieve greater success in their personal and professional lives.

Another important aspect of harnessing the power of positive thinking is to develop a growth mindset. A growth mindset is the belief that one's abilities and intelligence can be developed and improved through effort and learning. Individuals with a growth mindset are more likely to take on challenges, persist in the face of failure, and see setbacks as opportunities for growth and learning.

One way to develop a growth mindset is to challenge negative thoughts and beliefs. When faced with a negative thought or belief, such as "I can't do this" or "I'm not good enough," individuals can challenge these thoughts by asking themselves questions such as "What evidence do I have for this thought?" and "Is there a different way to think about this situation?" By questioning negative thoughts and beliefs, individuals can begin to shift their perspective and develop a more positive and growth-oriented mindset.

Another way to develop a growth mindset is to focus on progress rather than perfection. Perfectionism can lead to procrastination and a fear of failure, which can prevent individuals from taking action and achieving their goals. By focusing on progress rather than perfection, individuals can set realistic and attainable goals, take small steps towards achieving them, and see progress in their efforts.

It's also important to practice self-compassion. Self-compassion is the practice of being kind and understanding towards oneself, rather than being overly critical or self-judgmental. When individuals are self-compassionate, they are more likely to be resilient in the face of failure and setbacks, and are more likely to bounce back from difficult situations.

Finally, it's important to take care of one's physical and emotional well-being. Positive thinking and a positive attitude can help to improve one's overall well-being, but it's also important to take care of one's physical and emotional health. This includes getting enough sleep, eating a healthy diet, exercise, and engaging in activities that bring joy and relaxation.

In conclusion, harnessing the power of positive thinking is a powerful tool that can help individuals to achieve their goals, improve their mental and physical health, and lead happier, more fulfilling lives. By developing a growth mindset, challenging negative thoughts, focusing on progress, practicing self-compassion, and taking care of one's physical and emotional well-being, individuals can achieve greater success in their personal and professional lives. By incorporating positive thinking into one's daily routine and making it a habit, individuals can reap the benefits of positive thinking in their life.

16: Financial Empowerment

Financial empowerment is the process of gaining control over one's finances, including understanding and managing one's income, expenses, and investments. It is a crucial aspect of overall well-being and can have a significant impact on an individual's quality of life. In this chapter, we will explore the various elements of financial empowerment and discuss strategies for achieving it.

One of the first steps in achieving financial empowerment is understanding one's current financial situation. This includes analyzing one's income, expenses, and debts. It is important to have a clear understanding of where one's money is coming from and where it is going in order to develop a budget and create a plan for achieving financial goals. A budget is a financial plan that outlines how much money is expected to be earned and spent in a given period of time. It is a useful tool for managing finances and can help individuals stay on track with their financial goals.

Another key aspect of financial empowerment is understanding and managing debt. Debt can take many forms, including credit card debt, student loans, and mortgages. It is important to understand the terms and conditions of any debt, as well as the interest rates and fees associated with it. By understanding and managing debt, individuals can reduce the amount of money they owe and increase their overall financial stability.

Investing is another important aspect of financial empowerment. Investing allows individuals to grow their wealth and create financial security for the future. There are many different types of investments, including stocks, bonds, and real estate. It is important to understand the different types of investments and the risks and potential returns associated with them. A financial advisor can help individuals make informed investment decisions and create a diversified portfolio that aligns with their goals and risk tolerance.

Another important aspect of financial empowerment is having access to financial education and resources. Financial education can help individuals understand how to manage their money, invest, and plan for the future. There are many resources available, including books, online courses, and workshops. It is also important to be aware of financial scams and fraud, and to seek help if needed.

Finally, it is important to have a plan for achieving financial goals. This includes setting realistic and achievable goals, such as saving for a down payment on a house or retirement. A plan also includes setting a timeline for achieving these goals, and tracking progress along the way.

In conclusion, financial empowerment is an ongoing process that requires knowledge, understanding, and management of one's finances. By understanding one's current financial situation, managing debt, investing, and having access to financial education and resources, individuals can gain control over their finances and create financial stability and security for themselves and their families.

One important aspect of financial empowerment is having an emergency fund. An emergency fund is a savings account that is set aside for unexpected expenses such as medical bills, car repairs, or job loss. Having an emergency fund can provide a safety net and help individuals avoid going into debt in case of unexpected events. It is recommended to have at least three to six months' worth of living expenses saved in an emergency fund.

Another way to achieve financial empowerment is by automating your savings. It's easy to put off saving for the future, but by setting up automatic transfers from your checking account to your savings account, you can ensure that a portion of your income is set aside for future goals. This can be done on a weekly or monthly basis, depending on your preference.

Another important aspect of financial empowerment is learning how to negotiate. Whether it's negotiating a raise at work or haggling with a salesperson, the ability to negotiate can help individuals save money and increase their income. Learning how to effectively communicate your value and negotiate can pay off in the long run.

In order to achieve financial empowerment, it is also important to have a clear understanding of your credit score. Your credit score is a three-digit number that lenders use to determine your creditworthiness. It is based on factors such as your payment history, outstanding debt, and length of credit history. A good credit score can help you qualify for lower interest rates on loans, credit cards, and mortgages, which can save you thousands of dollars over time.

Finally, it is important to have a long-term perspective on your finances. This means thinking about the future and planning for it. This includes planning for retirement, saving for your children's education, and creating a will. It also means thinking about the impact of your financial decisions on future generations. By taking a long-term perspective on your finances, you can make better decisions today that will benefit you and your family in the future.

In conclusion, financial empowerment is a multifaceted process that involves understanding and managing one's finances, setting and achieving financial goals, and having access to financial education and resources. By taking control of your finances and making informed decisions, you can create financial stability and security for yourself and your family.

17: Empowering Your Career

Empowering Your Career

Your career is one of the most important aspects of your life. It not only provides you with financial stability and security, but it also gives you a sense of purpose and fulfillment. However, many people feel stuck in their careers and struggle to take control of their professional development. In this chapter, we will explore ways to empower your career and take charge of your professional journey.

The first step to empowering your career is to set clear and specific goals. Without a clear destination in mind, it can be difficult to know what steps to take to achieve success. Start by identifying your long-term career aspirations and then break them down into smaller, more manageable goals. For example, if your ultimate goal is to become a manager, your short-term goals may include taking on additional responsibilities, developing new skills, and networking with other professionals in your field.

Once you have set your goals, it is important to create a plan to achieve them. This may involve taking on new responsibilities, seeking out new opportunities, or developing new skills. It is also important to stay organized and track your progress. This will help you stay motivated and on track, and it will also help you identify any obstacles that may be preventing you from achieving your goals.

Another key aspect of empowering your career is networking. The connections you make with other professionals in your field can be incredibly valuable. They can provide you with opportunities for advancement, mentorship, and support. To build a strong professional network, you should attend industry events, join professional organizations, and connect with other professionals on LinkedIn.

In addition to networking, it is also important to invest in your own professional development. This may involve taking classes, attending workshops, or pursuing additional certifications. By continually learning and growing, you will be better equipped to take on new challenges and advance in your career.

Another important aspect of empowering your career is to be proactive and take initiative. This means not waiting for opportunities to come to you, but rather seeking them out and creating them yourself. This could mean pitching new ideas to your manager, starting a side hustle, or seeking out a mentor. By being proactive, you will be more likely to achieve your goals and take control of your career.

Another important aspect of empowering your career is to continuously improve your communication skills. Whether it is verbal or written, communication is key in building professional relationships and in making progress in any field. Being able to communicate effectively will enable you to clearly articulate your ideas, negotiate effectively, and build stronger relationships with your colleagues and superiors.

Finally, it is important to have a positive attitude and to maintain a sense of perspective. Having a positive attitude will help you stay motivated and focused on your goals, even when faced with obstacles. Additionally, it is important to remember that success is a journey, not a destination. Empowering your career is not about achieving a single goal or reaching a certain level of success, but about continuously working towards your goals and growing as a professional.

In conclusion, empowering your career is about taking charge of your professional development and actively working towards your goals. This involves setting clear and specific goals, creating a plan to achieve them, networking, investing in your own professional development, being proactive, continuously improving your communication skills and maintaining a positive attitude. Remember, success is a journey, not a destination, and by continually working towards your goals and growing as a professional, you will be able to empower your career and take control of your professional journey.

Another important aspect of empowering your career is to understand and leverage your strengths. Everyone has unique strengths and abilities that can be used to excel in their chosen field. By understanding and utilizing your strengths, you can find a career path that is fulfilling and that allows you to make the most impact.

To understand your strengths, you can take a strengths assessment or simply reflect on what you enjoy doing and what you are naturally good at. Once you have a clear understanding of your strengths, you can start to look for opportunities that align with them. This could mean pursuing a specific role within your current company or looking for a new job that utilizes your strengths.

Along with understanding and leveraging your strengths, it's also important to be adaptable and open to change. The job market and the economy are constantly changing, and it's important to be able to adapt to these changes in order to stay competitive. This means being open to new technologies, new ways of working, and new business models. By being adaptable, you will be more likely to find opportunities and be successful in your career.

Another important aspect of empowering your career is to build a personal brand. Your personal brand is the image or reputation that you have in the professional world. It's how others see you and what they think of when they think of you. Building a strong personal brand can help you stand out in your field, increase your visibility, and open up new opportunities.

To build a strong personal brand, you should focus on consistently delivering high-quality work, building relationships, and being a thought leader in your field. This can be done by writing articles, giving presentations, and speaking at industry events. Additionally, you should use social media and professional networks to promote your work, connect with others in your field, and share your thoughts and insights.

Finally, it is important to have a work-life balance. Having a balance between your professional and personal life is crucial for your well-being and overall satisfaction with your career. A work-life balance allows you to have enough time for your family, friends and hobbies, and also helps to reduce stress and burnout.

In conclusion, empowering your career is about taking charge of your professional development and actively working towards your goals. This involves setting clear and specific goals, creating a plan to achieve them, networking, investing in your own professional development, being proactive, continuously improving your communication skills, maintaining a positive attitude, understanding and leveraging your strengths, being adaptable and open to change, building a personal brand and having a work-life balance. Remember, career empowerment is a continuous process, and by consistently working on these areas, you will be able to take control of your professional journey and achieve the success you desire.

18: Conclusion: Living an Empowered Life

Living an empowered life is about taking control of your own destiny and making the most out of your experiences. It is about recognizing that you have the power to shape your own reality and that you have the ability to create the life you want for yourself.

Empowerment starts with self-awareness. To live an empowered life, you must first understand who you are, what you stand for, and what you want out of life. This requires taking a step back and looking at yourself objectively, without judgment or preconceived notions. It means being honest with yourself about your strengths and weaknesses, and understanding what drives you.

Once you have a clear understanding of yourself, you can begin to set goals and create a vision for your future. Setting goals is an important step in the empowerment process, as it gives you something to work towards and provides a sense of direction and purpose. These goals should be specific, measurable, and achievable, and should align with your values and what you want to achieve in life.

18: CONCLUSION: LIVING AN EMPOWERED LIFE

The next step in living an empowered life is to take action. This means putting in the work to achieve your goals and making things happen. It means taking risks and being willing to fail, as failure is an important part of the learning and growth process. It also means being proactive and taking responsibility for your actions, rather than waiting for things to happen to you.

Another important aspect of living an empowered life is developing a positive mindset. This means learning to see the good in every situation, and understanding that every challenge is an opportunity to grow and learn. It also means being resilient in the face of adversity, and having the ability to bounce back from setbacks and failures.

In addition to personal development, living an empowered life also means being a positive influence on those around you. This means being a role model for others, and inspiring them to live their best lives. It means being a leader and making a difference in the world.

Ultimately, living an empowered life is about being true to yourself and living in alignment with your values and what is most important to you. It is about taking control of your own life and creating the reality you want for yourself. It is a journey that requires self-awareness, goal-setting, action, a positive mindset, and a commitment to personal growth and making a difference in the world.

One key aspect of living an empowered life is learning to trust yourself and your abilities. This means having confidence in your decisions and not second-guessing yourself. It means being true to yourself, even when faced with criticism or opposition from others. Trusting yourself also means being willing to take risks and step out of your comfort zone. By taking risks, you will be faced with new challenges and will have the opportunity to learn and grow as a person.

Another important aspect of living an empowered life is developing a strong sense of self-worth. This means recognizing your own value and understanding that you are worthy of love, respect, and happiness. It means not allowing others to define your worth or value, and instead, taking ownership of your own self-worth.

In addition to self-worth, living an empowered life also means developing a strong sense of self-care. This means taking care of your physical, emotional, and mental well-being. It means making time for yourself and engaging in activities that bring you joy and fulfillment. It also means learning to set boundaries and saying no to things that don't align with your values or goals.

To live an empowered life, it's also important to surround yourself with positive people. Having a supportive community of friends and family can help provide encouragement, guidance and motivation on your journey. It's also important to surround yourself with people who inspire and empower you, who believe in you and your potential.

Living an empowered life also means being mindful of the way you communicate with others. This means being assertive, clear, and direct in your communication, and learning to speak your truth. It also means listening actively and being open-minded to the perspectives of others.

In conclusion, living an empowered life is about taking control of your own destiny, developing a strong sense of self-awareness, setting goals, taking action, having a positive mindset, and making a difference in the world. It's about being true to yourself and living in alignment with your values and what is most important to you. It requires personal growth and development, but also a strong sense of self-worth, self-care, and supportive community. Remember that it's a journey and not a destination and always strive to be the best version of yourself.

Book 2 - Overcome Trauma

A Comprehensive Guide to Understanding, Healing and Moving Forward from Past Trauma and Adversity, Including Techniques for Processing Traumatic Memories, Building Resilience, and Finding Empowerment

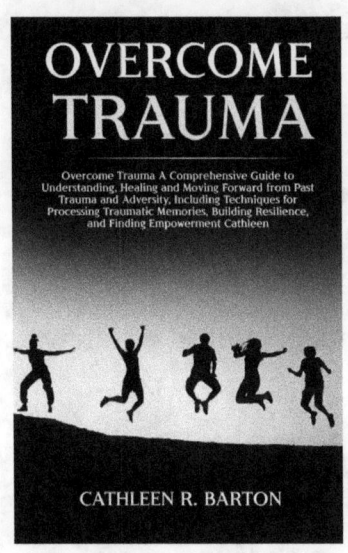

01: Introduction: Understanding Trauma and Its Impact

Trauma is a complex and multi-faceted phenomenon that can have a significant impact on an individual's physical, emotional, and mental well-being. It can manifest in a variety of ways, from physical injuries and illnesses to emotional and psychological distress. Understanding trauma and its impact is essential for addressing and treating the effects of traumatic experiences.

Trauma is defined as an event or series of events that threaten an individual's sense of safety, security, and well-being. It can be caused by a wide range of experiences, including physical and sexual abuse, neglect, natural disasters, war, terrorism, and accidents. Trauma can also result from witnessing or being a part of a traumatic event, such as a car crash or a mass shooting.

One of the key characteristics of trauma is that it can have a profound and long-lasting impact on an individual's emotional and mental well-being. Trauma can lead to a wide range of symptoms, including anxiety, depression, post-traumatic stress disorder (PTSD), and other emotional and behavioral disorders. These symptoms can be debilitating and can significantly interfere with an individual's ability to function in their daily life.

The impact of trauma can also be felt in the body, as trauma can lead to physical symptoms such as chronic pain, headaches, and gastrointestinal problems. Trauma can also contribute to the development of certain illnesses, such as heart disease, diabetes, and cancer.

Trauma can also have a significant impact on an individual's relationships and interactions with others. Trauma can lead to feelings of isolation, mistrust, and fear, which can make it difficult for an individual to form and maintain healthy relationships. Trauma can also lead to difficulties in communication and intimacy, which can further contribute to feelings of isolation and loneliness.

It is important to note that not everyone who experiences a traumatic event will develop symptoms of trauma. Factors such as an individual's coping mechanisms, support system, and overall resilience can play a role in determining the severity and duration of the impact of trauma.

Treatment for trauma is essential for addressing and managing the symptoms and effects of traumatic experiences. Treatment options can include therapy, medication, and other forms of support, such as support groups and self-care practices. It is important to work with a qualified professional to determine the best course of treatment for an individual's specific needs and circumstances.

In conclusion, trauma is a complex and multi-faceted phenomenon that can have a significant impact on an individual's physical, emotional, and mental well-being. Understanding trauma and its impact is essential for addressing and treating the effects of traumatic experiences. With proper treatment, individuals can learn to manage their symptoms and move towards a healthier and more fulfilling life.

It is also important to understand that trauma can be experienced differently by different individuals and groups. For example, marginalized and oppressed populations may be more likely to experience traumatic events and may also face additional barriers to accessing appropriate care. This highlights the importance of a culturally competent and trauma-informed approach to treating and supporting individuals who have experienced trauma.

Additionally, it is important to recognize that trauma can be intergenerational, meaning that the effects of trauma can be passed down through families and communities. This is particularly relevant in the case of historical trauma, such as the trauma experienced by Indigenous communities as a result of colonization and forced assimilation. Understanding the role of intergenerational trauma can be important in addressing and treating the effects of trauma.

In working with individuals who have experienced trauma, it is important to approach them with empathy, understanding, and non-judgment. Trauma can be a sensitive and difficult topic to discuss, and it is important to create a safe and supportive environment for individuals to share their experiences and feelings.

It is also important to recognize that healing from trauma is a process, and it may take time for an individual to fully recover. It is not a one-time event but a journey that requires patience, compassion and support.

In conclusion, understanding trauma and its impact is essential for effectively addressing and supporting individuals who have experienced traumatic events. This includes understanding the unique ways in which trauma can affect different individuals and groups, as well as the role of intergenerational trauma. It also includes approaching individuals with empathy, understanding, and a non-judgmental attitude, and recognizing that healing is a journey that requires patience and support.

02: The Trauma Response and Its Effects on the Mind and Body

Trauma is a powerful and often debilitating experience that can affect a person's mind and body in a number of ways. The trauma response is the set of physical and psychological reactions that occur in the aftermath of a traumatic event, and it can have a significant impact on a person's overall well-being.

The mind and body are closely connected, and trauma can affect both in a number of ways. Trauma can cause a range of psychological symptoms, such as anxiety, depression, and post-traumatic stress disorder (PTSD). These conditions can be difficult to cope with and can have a profound impact on a person's quality of life.

Trauma can also affect the body in a number of ways. For example, it can cause physical symptoms such as headaches, stomachaches, and muscle tension. These symptoms can be caused by the release of stress hormones, such as cortisol, in response to the traumatic event. Additionally, trauma can also lead to sleep disturbances, which can further contribute to physical and psychological symptoms.

02: THE TRAUMA RESPONSE AND ITS EFFECTS ON THE MIND AND BODY

The trauma response can also have long-term effects on a person's mind and body. For example, people who experience trauma may be more susceptible to developing chronic health conditions, such as heart disease or diabetes. This is because the stress response can have a negative impact on the body's immune system, making it more vulnerable to illness.

Trauma can also have a significant impact on a person's relationships and social interactions. People who have experienced trauma may have difficulty trusting others, and may struggle to form close relationships. This can lead to feelings of isolation and loneliness, which can further contribute to mental health problems.

There are a number of treatments available for people who have experienced trauma. One of the most effective is cognitive-behavioral therapy (CBT), which can help people to understand and cope with the thoughts and feelings that are associated with the trauma. Other therapies, such as eye movement desensitization and reprocessing (EMDR) and prolonged exposure therapy (PE), can also be helpful in treating trauma.

Medication can also be used to help people cope with the symptoms of trauma. Antidepressant medications, such as selective serotonin reuptake inhibitors (SSRIs), can be effective in treating depression and anxiety. Other medications, such as benzodiazepines, can be used to help people cope with insomnia and other sleep disturbances.

In addition to these treatments, it is also important for people who have experienced trauma to take care of themselves in other ways. This can include getting enough sleep, eating a healthy diet, and engaging in regular physical activity. This can help to reduce the physical symptoms of trauma and can also improve overall well-being.

In conclusion, trauma is a powerful and often debilitating experience that can affect a person's mind and body in a number of ways. The trauma response is the set of physical and psychological reactions that occur in the aftermath of a traumatic event, and it can have a significant impact on a person's overall well-being. There are a number of treatments available for people who have experienced trauma, including cognitive-behavioral therapy, eye movement desensitization and reprocessing and prolonged exposure therapy, medication and self-care practices. It is important for people who have experienced trauma to seek professional help and support so that they can cope with the symptoms of trauma and improve their overall well-being.

It is also important for individuals who have experienced trauma to have a support system in place. This can include family, friends, and support groups. Having people to talk to and share their experiences with can be a valuable source of comfort and understanding.

Another important aspect of trauma recovery is addressing any unresolved issues or traumas from the past. Trauma often has a ripple effect, and unresolved past traumas can contribute to the development of new traumas. By addressing these past traumas and resolving them, individuals can reduce the likelihood of developing new traumas or experiencing a re-traumatization.

It is also important to note that the trauma response and recovery process are unique to each individual. Some people may recover more quickly than others and some may have more severe symptoms. It is important to understand that recovery is not a linear process and that individuals may experience setbacks or relapses.

In summary, the trauma response and its effects on the mind and body can be severe and long-lasting. However, with the right treatment and support, individuals can learn to cope with the symptoms of trauma and improve their overall well-being. It is important for individuals who have experienced trauma to seek professional help and support, to build a support system, and to address any unresolved issues or past traumas. It's also important to understand that recovery is a unique process and should not be rushed or expect it to follow a linear pattern.

03: Types of Trauma and Adversity

Trauma and adversity come in many forms and can have a profound impact on an individual's mental and physical well-being. Understanding the different types of trauma and adversity can help in recognizing and addressing the effects they can have on a person's life.

One of the most commonly discussed types of trauma is that which arises from physical or sexual abuse. This can include both childhood and adult experiences of abuse, as well as domestic violence and sexual assault. The effects of abuse can be long-lasting and include symptoms such as depression, anxiety, and post-traumatic stress disorder (PTSD).

Another type of trauma that is often discussed is that which arises from experiencing or witnessing a traumatic event. This can include events such as natural disasters, terrorist attacks, or mass shootings. The effects of these types of trauma can also include symptoms such as depression, anxiety, and PTSD.

A less well-known but equally impactful type of trauma is that which arises from neglect or abandonment. This can include childhood experiences of neglect or abandonment by parents or caregivers, as well as neglect in adult relationships. The effects of neglect can include feelings of worthlessness, abandonment, and trust issues.

Adversity can also come in the form of chronic stressors such as poverty, discrimination, or long-term illness. These types of adversity can have a cumulative effect, leading to a range of mental and physical health problems.

Another type of adversity is vicarious trauma, which occurs when an individual is exposed to trauma through their work or occupation, such as a first responder, medical professional, or therapist. This can lead to symptoms of PTSD and other mental health issues.

It is important to note that not all individuals who experience trauma or adversity will develop mental health problems. However, it is important to be aware of the potential effects and to provide support and resources to those who may be struggling.

Treatment for trauma and adversity can include therapy, medication, and support groups. It's important to find a treatment approach that works best for the individual, as recovery and healing are unique to each person.

In conclusion, trauma and adversity come in many forms and can have a significant impact on an individual's well-being. Recognizing the different types of trauma and adversity and understanding the potential effects can help in providing support and resources to those who may be struggling. It is also important to remember that recovery and healing are unique to each person, and that a range of treatment options is available to support individuals in their journey towards healing.

Another important type of trauma to consider is complex trauma. This type of trauma occurs as a result of prolonged and repeated experiences of abuse, neglect, or other forms of maltreatment. This can include experiences such as growing up in a war-torn region or living in a chronically abusive household. The effects of complex trauma can be far-reaching and can include symptoms such as dissociation, self-harm, and difficulty forming healthy relationships.

Another type of trauma that is becoming increasingly recognized is developmental trauma. This type of trauma occurs as a result of disruptions or failures in the development of the brain and nervous system, which can occur due to adverse experiences in early childhood. This can include experiences such as neglect, abuse, or exposure to violence. The effects of developmental trauma can include difficulties with regulation of emotions and behavior, as well as difficulties with attachment and relationships.

Trauma and adversity can also occur as a result of a traumatic loss, such as the death of a loved one or the loss of a limb. This type of trauma can be incredibly difficult to process and can lead to symptoms of depression and grief.

Lastly, it's important to recognize that trauma and adversity can also occur within the context of one's culture or community. This can include experiences such as discrimination, racism, or cultural dislocation. The effects of this type of trauma can include feelings of alienation, cultural confusion and identity issues.

In summary, trauma and adversity can take on many forms, and it's important to consider the unique experiences of each individual. While some types of trauma are more well-known and discussed, such as physical and sexual abuse, other forms of trauma, such as complex trauma, developmental trauma, cultural trauma and traumatic loss, are equally impactful and deserve attention and support. It's crucial to understand the different types of trauma and adversity so that individuals can receive the appropriate support and resources to promote healing and recovery.

04: The Trauma Healing Process: Understanding the Stages of Recovery

Trauma is a deeply distressing or disturbing event that can have a lasting impact on an individual's mental, emotional, and physical well-being. The trauma healing process is a journey that can take time and requires patience, understanding, and support. It is important to understand that everyone's experience of trauma is unique and their healing journey will be different. However, there are some general stages of recovery that are commonly recognized in the trauma healing process.

The first stage of the trauma healing process is the acute stage. This stage is characterized by feelings of shock, disbelief, and numbness. The individual may have difficulty processing what has happened and may have trouble sleeping, eating, or engaging in daily activities. They may also experience physical symptoms such as headaches, muscle tension, and fatigue.

The second stage of the trauma healing process is the denial stage. This stage is characterized by a refusal to acknowledge or accept the reality of the trauma. The individual may try to deny that the trauma occurred or may minimize the impact it has had on their life. They may also try to avoid thinking or talking about the trauma.

The third stage of the trauma healing process is the anger stage. This stage is characterized by feelings of anger, resentment, and frustration. The individual may be angry at themselves, the perpetrator, or others who were involved in the trauma. They may also feel that the trauma is unfair or unjust.

The fourth stage of the trauma healing process is the bargaining stage. This stage is characterized by a feeling of helplessness and a desire to regain control. The individual may try to make deals with themselves or with a higher power in an attempt to undo or change the trauma. They may also try to find meaning in the trauma by searching for a lesson to be learned.

The fifth stage of the trauma healing process is the depression stage. This stage is characterized by feelings of sadness, hopelessness, and despair. The individual may have difficulty finding pleasure in things they used to enjoy and may have trouble sleeping or eating. They may also feel guilty, ashamed, or responsible for the trauma.

The sixth stage of the trauma healing process is the acceptance stage. This stage is characterized by a recognition and acceptance of the reality of the trauma. The individual may have a renewed sense of hope and may begin to move forward in their life. They may also begin to find new ways to cope with the trauma and to find meaning in their experience.

It's important to note that these stages are not linear, and a person may revisit different stages at different times or may not go through all of the stages. Additionally, some people may experience long-term psychological symptoms, such as post-traumatic stress disorder (PTSD) and may need additional support and treatment. It's also important to note that healing is a unique and personal process that may take different form for each individual.

In conclusion, the trauma healing process is a journey that can take time and requires patience, understanding, and support. It is important to understand that everyone's experience of trauma is unique and their healing journey will

be different. However, by understanding the stages of recovery, it can help individuals better understand their own
healing journey and provide them with the support they
need to move forward. It's also important to seek professional help if needed and never feel ashamed to reach out
for support.

It's also important to note that the trauma healing process
can be different for different individuals. Some people may
find traditional therapy, such as cognitive-behavioral therapy, to be helpful in their healing journey. Others may find
alternative therapies, such as art therapy or mindfulness-
based practices, to be more beneficial. It's important for individuals to explore different options and find what works
best for them.

Another important aspect of the trauma healing process is
self-care. Taking care of oneself physically, emotionally, and
mentally is crucial in the healing process. This may include
things such as exercise, healthy eating, getting enough
sleep, and engaging in activities that bring joy and relaxation. It's also important to practice self-compassion and be
kind to oneself during this journey.

04: THE TRAUMA HEALING PROCESS: UNDERSTANDING THE STAGES OF RECOVERY

It's important to remember that healing from trauma is not a one-time event. It's a continuous process that may take time, and individuals may experience setbacks along the way. It's important to be patient with oneself and to recognize that healing is not a linear process. It's also important to understand that healing is not the same as forgetting or erasing the trauma. It's about learning to live with the trauma and finding ways to cope with it.

In addition to individual therapy and self-care, support from friends, family, and loved ones is an important aspect of the trauma healing process. Having people to talk to and share the journey with can be incredibly helpful. It's also important for loved ones to be patient and understanding during the healing process, as well as educate themselves about trauma and its effects.

In conclusion, the trauma healing process is a journey that takes time, patience, and support. It's important to understand that everyone's experience of trauma is unique and their healing journey will be different. However, by understanding the stages of recovery, exploring different therapy options, practicing self-care and having a support system, individuals can find ways to heal and move forward in their lives. Remember that healing is not a one-time event, it's an ongoing process and it's important to be kind to yourself and to seek help if needed.

05: The Importance of Self-Care in Trauma Recovery

Self-care is a critical component of the healing process for individuals who have experienced trauma. Trauma can take many forms, from physical abuse to emotional neglect, and can have a profound impact on an individual's mental and physical well-being. The effects of trauma can be long-lasting and can manifest in a variety of ways, including depression, anxiety, and post-traumatic stress disorder (PTSD).

Self-care is a way for individuals to take control of their own healing and to actively work towards recovery. It involves engaging in activities that promote physical and mental well-being, such as exercise, healthy eating, and stress-management techniques. It also includes taking time for oneself, setting boundaries, and learning to say no to demands that may be overwhelming.

One of the most important aspects of self-care is understanding and acknowledging the impact of trauma on one's life. This means being honest with oneself about the ways in which trauma has affected one's thoughts, feelings, and behaviors. It also means acknowledging the impact of trauma on relationships and recognizing the need for support from others.

Self-care also involves learning to cope with the symptoms of trauma, such as flashbacks and nightmares. This can be done through a variety of methods, such as cognitive-behavioral therapy, mindfulness techniques, and medication. In addition, self-care includes taking steps to manage stress and to build resilience, such as exercise, yoga, and meditation.

Self-care also involves learning to set boundaries and to take time for oneself. This means saying no to demands that may be overwhelming and setting limits on the amount of time and energy one is willing to give to others. It also means learning to set boundaries with oneself, such as setting realistic goals and taking time to rest and relax.

Self-care also involves taking care of one's physical health. This includes getting enough sleep, eating a healthy diet, and engaging in regular physical activity. It also means paying attention to physical symptoms that may be related to trauma and seeking medical attention when necessary.

Finally, self-care involves reaching out for help and support when needed. This may include talking to a therapist or counselor, joining a support group, or talking to friends and family. It is important to remember that healing from trauma is a process and that it is not something that can be done alone.

In conclusion, self-care is an essential component of trauma recovery. It involves taking control of one's own healing, acknowledging the impact of trauma, learning to cope with symptoms, setting boundaries, taking care of one's physical health, and reaching out for help and support. It is a ongoing process of self-discovery and self-care that is essential for individuals who have experienced trauma to live a fulfilling life.

Self-care is not a one-time event, but a continuous process that requires ongoing effort and commitment. It is important to remember that healing from trauma is not a linear process and that there will be setbacks and challenges along the way. It is important to be patient with oneself and to recognize that progress may be slow.

It is also important to recognize that self-care is not just about taking care of oneself, but also about understanding

and addressing the societal and cultural factors that contribute to trauma. For example, recognizing and addressing
the impact of racism, poverty, and discrimination on mental
health and well-being is an important aspect of self-care for
marginalized communities.

In order to practice self-care, it is important to make a plan
and to set achievable goals. This may include setting aside
time each day for self-care activities, such as exercise or
meditation, or setting a goal to attend a certain number of
therapy sessions each month. It may also include making a
list of self-care activities that are enjoyable and meaningful,
such as reading a book or taking a relaxing bath.

It is also important to be mindful of self-care practices that
may be harmful or unproductive, such as substance abuse
or avoiding responsibilities. These practices may provide
temporary relief, but they ultimately perpetuate the negative effects of trauma and can lead to further harm in the
long run.

In addition, self-care also includes seeking professional
help, such as counseling or therapy, when needed. A trained
therapist can help individuals understand and cope with the

effects of trauma, as well as provide tools and strategies for self-care and healing.

In conclusion, self-care is an essential aspect of the healing process for individuals who have experienced trauma. It involves acknowledging the impact of trauma, learning to cope with symptoms, setting boundaries, taking care of one's physical health, and reaching out for help and support. It is a ongoing process of self-discovery and self-care that requires patience, effort, and commitment. Additionally, it is important to recognize the societal and cultural factors that contribute to trauma and to address them. Remember that healing is a journey, and it is not something that can be rushed or forced, but rather it is something that one should take the time to nurture and care for.

06: Processing Traumatic Memories: Techniques and Strategies

Traumatic memories can have a significant impact on an individual's mental health and well-being. These memories are often vivid, distressing, and can be triggered by seemingly insignificant cues in the individual's environment. Processing traumatic memories is an essential step in healing and moving forward. In this chapter, we will discuss techniques and strategies for processing traumatic memories.

One of the most effective techniques for processing traumatic memories is cognitive-behavioral therapy (CBT). CBT is a form of psychotherapy that focuses on the relationship between thoughts, feelings, and behaviors. The goal of CBT is to help individuals identify and change negative thought patterns and beliefs that may be preventing them from moving on from their traumatic experiences.

One technique used in CBT is exposure therapy. Exposure therapy involves gradually confronting the traumatic memories in a controlled and safe environment. The individual will be asked to describe their traumatic memory in detail, including their thoughts and feelings at the time. The

therapist will then help the individual challenge any negative thoughts and beliefs that may be associated with the
memory. Over time, as the individual becomes more comfortable with the memory, they will be able to think about it
without feeling overwhelmed.

Another technique used in CBT is cognitive restructuring.
This technique involves identifying and challenging negative thoughts and beliefs associated with the traumatic
memory. The individual will be asked to identify their automatic thoughts and beliefs and to challenge them with more
realistic and balanced thoughts. This can help the individual
to see the traumatic event in a different light and to develop
a more positive perspective.

A different strategy is Eye Movement Desensitization and
Reprocessing (EMDR). EMDR is a form of psychotherapy
that uses bilateral stimulation, such as eye movements, to
process traumatic memories. The therapist will guide the
individual to recall their traumatic memory while engaging
in the bilateral stimulation. The theory is that the bilateral
stimulation helps to process the traumatic memory, making
it less distressing.

Another strategy is Mindfulness-based therapy. Mindfulness-based therapy involves learning to be present in the
moment and to focus on one's thoughts and feelings
without judgment. This can help individuals to become
more aware of their thoughts and feelings and to develop a
sense of acceptance and understanding. Mindfulness-based
therapy can be used in conjunction with other techniques to
help individuals process traumatic memories.

Another strategy is Relaxation techniques. Relaxation techniques such as deep breathing, progressive muscle relaxation, and visualization can help individuals to reduce their
emotional distress and physical tension. Relaxation techniques can be used to help individuals calm down when
they are feeling overwhelmed by traumatic memories.

It's important to note that processing traumatic memories
can be a difficult and emotional process, and it's important
to have a support system in place. This may include friends,
family, or a therapist. It's also important to remember that
healing is a process and it may take time.

In conclusion, processing traumatic memories is an important step in healing and moving forward. There are various

techniques and strategies that can be used to help individuals process traumatic memories, including cognitive-behavioral therapy, exposure therapy, cognitive restructuring,
Eye Movement Desensitization and Reprocessing, mindfulness-based therapy and relaxation techniques. It's important to work with a therapist or counselor and to have a support system in place while processing traumatic memories.
Remember to be patient and compassionate with yourself as
healing can take time.

Another strategy for processing traumatic memories is to
use creative outlets such as art, writing, or music. These
outlets can provide a way for individuals to express their
thoughts and feelings about their traumatic experiences
without the need for words. This can be especially helpful
for individuals who may have difficulty verbalizing their
thoughts and feelings.

Art therapy, for example, is a form of therapy that uses art
materials such as paint, clay, or collage to help individuals
express their thoughts and feelings. The therapist will guide
the individual to create art that represents their traumatic
experience, and will then help the individual to explore

their thoughts and feelings about the art.

Writing therapy, also known as journaling, is a form of therapy that involves writing about one's thoughts and feelings. The therapist will guide the individual to write about their traumatic experience, and will then help the individual to explore their thoughts and feelings about the experience.

Music therapy is a form of therapy that uses music to help individuals express their thoughts and feelings. The therapist will guide the individual to listen to music that represents their traumatic experience, and will then help the individual to explore their thoughts and feelings about the music.

It's important to note that these creative outlets should be used in conjunction with other techniques, such as cognitive-behavioral therapy or exposure therapy. They can be an additional tool to help individuals process their traumatic memories.

In addition to the above strategies, it's also important to take care of oneself while processing traumatic memories. This includes getting enough sleep, eating a healthy diet, and engaging in regular physical activity. These self-care practices can help to reduce stress and promote overall well-being.

In conclusion, processing traumatic memories is a difficult but necessary process in order to move forward and heal. There are various techniques and strategies that can be used to help individuals process traumatic memories, such as cognitive-behavioral therapy, exposure therapy, cognitive restructuring, Eye Movement Desensitization and Reprocessing, mindfulness-based therapy, relaxation techniques, and creative outlets such as art, writing, and music therapy. It's important to work with a therapist or counselor and to have a support system in place while processing traumatic memories. Additionally, self-care practices such as getting enough sleep, eating a healthy diet, and engaging in regular physical activity can also play an important role in promoting overall well-being. Remember to be patient and compassionate with yourself as healing can take time.

07: Building Resilience: How to Develop a Stronger Mind and Spirit

Building resilience is the ability to bounce back from adversity and to maintain a positive outlook in the face of difficult circumstances. It is a combination of mental, emotional, and physical strength that enables individuals to cope with stress and adversity, and to emerge from difficult situations stronger and more capable than before. Resilience is an important skill to develop, as it can help you to overcome challenges and to live a more fulfilling life.

There are several key strategies that you can use to develop resilience and to build a stronger mind and spirit. These strategies include:

– Setting realistic goals: Setting realistic goals is one of the most effective ways to build resilience. When you set goals that are achievable and that align with your values, you are more likely to feel motivated and energized by the process of working towards them. This can help you to maintain a positive outlook and to persevere through difficult times.

– Practicing mindfulness: Mindfulness is the practice of being present in the moment and paying attention to your thoughts, feelings, and sensations without judgment. It can help you to develop resilience by enabling you to stay focused on the present moment and to avoid getting bogged down by negative thoughts and emotions.

– Building a support network: Building a support network of friends, family, and professionals can help you to build resilience by providing you with a sense of connection and belonging. When you feel supported, you are more likely to feel confident and capable of facing challenges.

– Engaging in physical activity: Engaging in regular physical activity is one of the most effective ways to build resilience. Exercise releases endorphins, which are chemicals that can make you feel happier and more energized. Additionally, regular exercise can help to improve your overall physical health, which can in turn help to boost your mental and emotional well-being.

– Fostering a positive attitude: Fostering a positive attitude is one of the most effective ways to build resilience. When you focus on the good things in your life and practice gratitude, you are more likely to feel positive and optimistic about your future. Additionally, when you practice positive thinking, you can help to counteract the negative thoughts and emotions that can hold you back.

– Give back to community and help others: Giving back to community and helping others can help to build resilience by providing a sense of purpose and meaning. When you are able to make a positive impact on the world, you are more likely to feel fulfilled and satisfied with your life. Additionally, helping others can take the focus off of your own problems, which can help to reduce stress and anxiety.

In conclusion, building resilience is an ongoing process that requires time and effort, but the benefits are well worth it. By setting realistic goals, practicing mindfulness, building a support network, engaging in physical activity, fostering a positive attitude and giving back to community, you can develop a stronger mind and spirit that will help you to cope with stress and adversity, and to live a more fulfilling life. Remember that resilience is not about never experiencing difficulties, it's about being able to handle them and find the opportunities in them.

– Learning from failure: Failure is an inevitable part of life, and it is important to learn from it rather than dwelling on it. When you fail, it is important to take the time to reflect on what went wrong and what you can do differently next time. This can help you to build resilience by teaching you valuable lessons and helping you to grow as a person.

– Developing a growth mindset: Having a growth mindset means embracing challenges and seeing them as opportunities for growth. When you have a growth mindset, you are more likely to take risks and to view failure as a learning opportunity. This can help you to build resilience by teaching you to be more adaptable and to view challenges as opportunities for growth.

– Taking care of yourself: Taking care of yourself is crucial for building resilience. This means taking care of your physical, emotional and mental health. Eating a healthy diet, getting enough sleep, practicing self-care and managing stress are all important for maintaining good overall health.

– Seek professional help when needed: If you are struggling to build resilience on your own, it may be helpful to seek professional help. A therapist or counselor can help you to work through difficult emotions and to develop strategies for coping with stress and adversity. They can also help you to identify and address any underlying issues that may be contributing to your difficulties.

In conclusion, building resilience is a lifelong process that requires time and effort, but the benefits are well worth it. By setting realistic goals, practicing mindfulness, building a support network, engaging in physical activity, fostering a positive attitude, giving back to community, learning from failure, developing a growth mindset, taking care of yourself and seeking professional help when needed, you can develop a stronger mind and spirit that will help you to cope with stress and adversity, and to live a more fulfilling life. Remember that resilience is not about never experiencing difficulties, it's about being able to handle them and find the opportunities in them.

08: Finding Empowerment: How to Take Control of Your Trauma Narrative

Introduction

Trauma can be a devastating and debilitating experience, leaving those who have gone through it feeling lost, alone, and without control. However, it is possible to take control of your trauma narrative and find empowerment in the aftermath. This chapter will explore some of the ways you can take control of your trauma narrative, including understanding your trauma, facing your feelings, and finding support.

Understanding Your Trauma

The first step to taking control of your trauma narrative is to understand what trauma is and how it has affected you. Trauma is a deeply distressing or disturbing event that can have lasting effects on a person's mental, emotional, and physical well-being. It can be caused by a variety of events, such as physical or emotional abuse, sexual assault, natural disasters, or the loss of a loved one.

08: FINDING EMPOWERMENT: HOW TO TAKE CONTROL OF YOUR TRAUMA NARRATIVE

It is important to understand that everyone's experience of trauma is unique, and there is no "right" or "wrong" way to feel. You may feel a range of emotions, including anger, fear, guilt, and sadness. You may also experience physical symptoms such as headaches, fatigue, and difficulty sleeping. It is important to acknowledge and accept these feelings, rather than trying to push them away or ignore them.

Facing Your Feelings

Once you have a better understanding of your trauma and how it has affected you, it is important to face your feelings head-on. This may mean talking to a therapist or counselor, writing in a journal, or talking to a trusted friend or family member. It is important to find a way to express your feelings that feels safe and comfortable for you.

It is also important to remember that healing is a process, and it may take time. You may have setbacks, and that's okay. It's important to be patient with yourself and to remember that you are not alone in your journey.

Finding Support

08: FINDING EMPOWERMENT: HOW TO TAKE CONTROL OF YOUR TRAUMA NARRATIVE

One of the most important things you can do to take control of your trauma narrative is to find support. This can come in many forms, including therapy, counseling, support groups, or even online communities. It is important to find a support system that feels safe and comfortable for you.

It is also important to surround yourself with people who understand and support you. This may mean cutting ties with people who are not supportive or who may be triggering to you. It is important to remember that you deserve to be surrounded by people who care about you and want to help you heal.

Conclusion

Taking control of your trauma narrative can be a difficult and challenging process, but it is possible. By understanding your trauma, facing your feelings, and finding support, you can begin to take control of your story and find empowerment in the aftermath. Remember to be patient with yourself, and to surround yourself with people who care about you and want to help you heal. With time and support, you can come to a place of peace and acceptance.

08: FINDING EMPOWERMENT: HOW TO TAKE CON-TROL OF YOUR TRAUMA NARRATIVE

Another important aspect of taking control of your trauma narrative is to learn how to manage and cope with the symptoms that may result from your trauma. This may include things like anxiety, depression, and flashbacks. It is important to educate yourself about these symptoms and to learn ways to manage them. This can include things like mindfulness techniques, cognitive-behavioral therapy, and medication. It is also important to find a support system that can help you manage your symptoms, whether that be a therapist, counselor, or support group.

Another important aspect of taking control of your trauma narrative is to find ways to take care of yourself. Self-care is crucial for healing, and it can include things like exercise, eating a healthy diet, getting enough sleep, and engaging in activities that you enjoy. It is also important to find ways to relax and de-stress, such as yoga, meditation, or listening to music.

In addition, it's important to be open to the idea of forgiveness, both for yourself and for others. Forgiveness is not about forgetting or excusing the hurt that was done, but it's about accepting that it happened, and not allowing it to continue to control you. It is a process and it can take time, but it is worth it in the end.

Finally, it is important to remember that you are not defined by your trauma. You are not a victim, you are a survivor. You have the strength and resilience to overcome what you have been through, and to live a fulfilling and meaningful life. You are capable of finding empowerment and taking control of your trauma narrative.

In conclusion, Finding empowerment after a traumatic event is a journey and it can be hard and take time, but it is important to understand your trauma, to face your feelings, to find support and to learn how to cope with the symptoms that may result from your trauma, to take care of yourself, to learn forgiveness, and to remember that you are not defined by your trauma. With time and support, you can come to a place of peace and acceptance and start to take control of your narrative and empower yourself.

09: Navigating Support Systems: Finding Help and Resources

Navigating Support Systems: Finding Help and Resources

When dealing with difficult situations, it can be overwhelming to try and find the right resources and support. Whether you are facing a personal crisis, dealing with mental health issues, or trying to navigate the healthcare system, it can be hard to know where to turn for help. In this chapter, we will explore some strategies for finding the support and resources you need to get through tough times.

First, it is important to understand that there is no one-size-fits-all solution when it comes to finding support. Different people may need different types of help and resources depending on their specific situation. However, there are some general tips and strategies that can be helpful when trying to find the right support for you.

One important strategy is to do your research. There are many different types of support and resources available, so it can be helpful to take the time to learn about the different options that are available. This can include things like therapy, support groups, and healthcare services. By researching different options, you can get a better sense of what might be the best fit for your needs.

Another important strategy is to reach out to people you trust. This can include friends, family members, and other loved ones who can provide you with emotional support and guidance. They may also be able to provide you with information about different resources and support systems that they have used in the past.

You can also seek out professional help. You can talk to a therapist, counselor, or other mental health professional who can provide you with guidance and support. They can help you work through your feelings and develop coping strategies that can help you get through difficult times. They can also help you navigate the healthcare system and find the right resources for your needs.

Additionally, many organizations, such as non-profits and government agencies, provide a wide range of services and support to those who need it. You can contact these organizations directly and ask about the services they offer. They can provide you with information about programs and services that may be able to help you.

In addition, many communities have helplines that provide a wide range of support services and resources. They can provide you with information about local services and resources and connect you with the right people who can help.

It is also important to know your rights. This can include understanding your rights as a patient and your rights to access healthcare services and other types of support. Knowing your rights can help you advocate for yourself and get the help you need.

Finally, it is important to remember that you are not alone. There are many people who are going through similar situations and who have been able to find the support and resources they need to get through tough times. It may take some time and effort to find the right resources and support, but with persistence and determination, you can get the help you need.

In conclusion, finding the right support and resources can be a challenging task, but with the right strategies, you can navigate the support systems and find the help you need. It is important to do your research, reach out to people you trust, seek professional help, and know your rights. Remember that you are not alone and that with persistence, you can get the help you need to get through difficult times.

It's also important to be open to trying different types of support and resources. What works for one person may not work for another, so it's important to be willing to try different options and find what works best for you. This may include therapy, medication, support groups, and other types of resources.

Another important aspect of navigating support systems is being aware of cultural and language barriers. If English is not your first language, or if you come from a different cultural background, it may be difficult to find resources and support that are tailored to your specific needs. In this case, it may be helpful to seek out resources and support that are culturally and linguistically appropriate. This may include organizations that serve specific ethnic and linguistic communities or translation services that can help you communicate with healthcare providers and other types of support.

It's also important to be aware of financial barriers when seeking help and resources. Many support systems and resources require payment, and this can be a barrier for some people. If you are unable to afford the support or resources you need, it may be helpful to seek out organizations that provide financial assistance or programs that can help you pay for the support and resources you need.

Finally, it's important to remember that seeking help and resources is not a sign of weakness. It takes courage and strength to admit that you need help, and it's important to remember that everyone goes through difficult times and needs support. Seeking help and resources is a sign of resilience and the determination to improve your well-being.

In conclusion, navigating support systems can be a challenging task, but with the right strategies and information, you can find the help and resources you need to get through difficult times. It's important to do your research, reach out to people you trust, seek professional help, and know your rights. Remember to be open to trying different types of support, be aware of cultural and language barriers, and financial barriers, and remember that seeking help is a sign of strength and resilience.

10: Trauma and Relationships: How Trauma Can Affect Connections with Others

Trauma can have a profound impact on an individual's ability to form and maintain healthy relationships. Traumatic experiences, such as physical or emotional abuse, neglect, or exposure to violence, can disrupt the development of secure attachment patterns, affect the way a person sees themselves and others, and influence the way they cope with stress and negative emotions. As a result, trauma survivors may struggle to trust, communicate effectively, and form intimate connections with others.

One of the most significant ways that trauma can affect relationships is through the development of insecure attachment patterns. Secure attachment patterns develop when a child feels safe and secure in their relationship with their primary caregiver, and as a result, they learn to trust and rely on others. However, when a child experiences trauma, such as abuse or neglect, they may learn that the people they depend on for survival are not trustworthy or safe. As a result, they may develop insecure attachment patterns, such as avoidant or anxious attachment styles.

10: TRAUMA AND RELATIONSHIPS: HOW TRAUMA CAN AFFECT CONNECTIONS WITH OTHERS

Individuals with avoidant attachment styles tend to avoid intimacy and close relationships, often pushing people away to protect themselves from potential hurt or rejection. They may have difficulty trusting others and may struggle to form deep emotional connections. On the other hand, individuals with anxious attachment styles may crave intimacy and close relationships, but may struggle to trust others and may have difficulty setting healthy boundaries. They may also experience intense feelings of insecurity and fear of abandonment.

Trauma can also affect the way a person sees themselves and others. Trauma survivors may develop negative self-perceptions, such as feeling guilty, ashamed, or worthless. They may also struggle to trust their own perceptions and may doubt their ability to make healthy decisions. As a result, they may have difficulty setting healthy boundaries and may struggle to assert themselves in relationships.

Additionally, trauma can influence the way a person copes with stress and negative emotions. Trauma survivors may develop unhealthy coping mechanisms, such as substance abuse, self-harm, or avoidance. These coping mechanisms can interfere with the ability to form and maintain healthy relationships. For example, substance abuse can lead to problems with communication, trust, and intimacy, while avoidance can interfere with the ability to resolve conflicts and work through problems.

Furthermore, trauma can also lead to the development of certain mental health conditions, such as PTSD or depression, which can further affect relationships. Symptoms of PTSD, such as flashbacks and hypervigilance, can make it difficult for the person to relax and feel safe in close relationships. Depression can lead to feelings of worthlessness, hopelessness and lack of energy, making it hard for the person to engage in social interactions and maintain relationships.

It's important to note that trauma can affect different people in different ways and it's not possible to predict how someone will react to traumatic events. However, there are several ways to help individuals who have experienced trauma to build and maintain healthy relationships. One of the most effective ways is through therapy, such as cognitive-behavioral therapy, which can help individuals to identify and challenge negative thoughts and beliefs, develop healthy coping mechanisms, and improve communication skills.

Another effective way is through trauma-focused therapy, such as Eye Movement Desensitization and Reprocessing (EMDR) which aims to process and heal traumatic memories, so the person can live a life that is less affected by traumatic memories. Trauma-focused therapy can also help individuals to develop a sense of safety, trust, and connection with others.

It's important for the person's support system, family, and friends to be understanding and supportive of the person's healing process. It's also important for them to educate themselves about trauma and its effects on relationships, in order to provide the right kind of support.

In conclusion, trauma can have a significant impact on an individual's ability to form and maintain healthy relationships. Trauma survivors may struggle with trust, communication, and intimacy due to the development of insecure attachment patterns, negative self-perceptions, and unhealthy coping mechanisms. Additionally, trauma can also lead to the development of certain mental health conditions, such as PTSD or depression, which can further affect relationships.

However, there are ways to help individuals who have experienced trauma to build and maintain healthy relationships. Therapy, such as cognitive-behavioral therapy and trauma-focused therapy, can help individuals to identify and challenge negative thoughts and beliefs, develop healthy coping mechanisms, and improve communication skills. It's also important for the person's support system, family, and friends to be understanding and supportive of the person's healing process and educate themselves about trauma and its effects on relationships.

It's essential to remember that healing and recovery from trauma is a process and it takes time. It's important to be patient and compassionate with oneself and others who have experienced trauma, and to keep in mind that healing and forming healthy relationships is possible.

11: Trauma and Mental Health: Understanding the Connection

Trauma and mental health are closely connected, as experiences of trauma can have a profound impact on an individual's mental well-being. Trauma refers to a wide range of experiences, including physical and emotional abuse, neglect, natural disasters, and military combat. The effects of trauma can be long-lasting and can manifest in a variety of ways, including anxiety, depression, and post-traumatic stress disorder (PTSD).

When an individual experiences a traumatic event, their brain and body respond in a way that is designed to protect them from harm. The body's "fight or flight" response is activated, releasing hormones such as adrenaline and cortisol that help the individual respond to the threat. This response can be helpful in the immediate aftermath of a traumatic event, as it allows the individual to take action to protect themselves. However, if the trauma is not resolved, the individual may continue to experience the symptoms of this response, such as increased heart rate, difficulty sleeping, and difficulty concentrating.

For some individuals, the effects of trauma may not become

apparent until weeks, months, or even years after the event. This is particularly true for individuals who have experienced complex trauma, such as ongoing abuse or neglect. Complex trauma is characterized by repeated and prolonged exposure to traumatic events, and it can have a particularly devastating impact on an individual's mental health.

One of the most common mental health conditions associated with trauma is PTSD. This condition is characterized by a range of symptoms, including intrusive thoughts or memories of the traumatic event, avoidance of people, places, or activities that remind the individual of the trauma, and feelings of hypervigilance or increased arousal. Individuals with PTSD may also experience flashbacks or nightmares, and they may feel detached or emotionally numb.

Another common condition that can develop as a result of trauma is depression. Trauma can be a significant risk factor for the development of depression, and individuals who have experienced trauma may be more likely to experience feelings of hopelessness, helplessness, and worthlessness. They may also have difficulty sleeping, lose interest in activities that they once enjoyed, and have difficulty concentrating.

Anxiety disorders are also commonly associated with trauma. Trauma can cause individuals to feel constantly on edge, and they may experience physical symptoms such as a racing heart or difficulty breathing. They may also experience feelings of panic and fear, and they may avoid certain people, places, or activities that remind them of the trauma.

In addition to these specific mental health conditions, trauma can also impact an individual's overall well-being. Individuals who have experienced trauma may have difficulty trusting others, and they may have difficulty forming and maintaining healthy relationships. They may also have difficulty regulating their emotions, and they may experience feelings of shame or guilt.

It's important to note that not everyone who experiences trauma will develop mental health problems. Resilience and support from loved ones and mental health professionals can play a key role in helping individuals to cope with the effects of trauma. However, for many individuals, professional help is necessary to process and heal from the trauma.

Treatment for trauma-related mental health conditions typically involves talk therapy, such as cognitive-behavioral therapy (CBT) or eye movement desensitization and reprocessing (EMDR). These therapies can help individuals to process their traumatic experiences, learn to manage their symptoms, and develop coping strategies. Medications, such as antidepressants, may also be prescribed to help manage symptoms of depression and anxiety.

In conclusion, trauma and mental health are closely connected, and experiences of trauma can have a profound impact on an individual's mental well-being. Trauma can lead to a wide range of mental health problems, including PTSD, depression, and anxiety disorders. It's important to for individuals who have experienced trauma to receive professional help in order to process and heal from their experiences. Treatment for trauma-related mental health conditions typically involves talk therapy and medication, and can help individuals to manage their symptoms and develop coping strategies. It's also important for individuals, friends and families to understand the connection between trauma and mental health, in order to recognize the symptoms and seek help early on.

Additionally, it's important to address the societal and systemic issues that can lead to trauma, such as poverty, discrimination, and lack of access to resources. Addressing these issues can help to reduce the prevalence of trauma and improve mental health outcomes for individuals and communities.

It's important to remember that healing from trauma is a process, and it can take time. But with the right support and resources, individuals can learn to manage their symptoms and move forward in their lives. It's important to be patient with yourself and to seek help if you're struggling with the effects of trauma.

12: Trauma and Addiction: How Trauma Can Lead to Substance Abuse

Trauma and addiction are closely intertwined. Trauma can lead to substance abuse as a way of coping with overwhelming emotions and memories. Conversely, substance abuse can also lead to further trauma, creating a cycle that can be difficult to break. In this chapter, we will explore the relationship between trauma and addiction and how understanding this connection can aid in the treatment of both conditions.

Trauma is defined as a deeply distressing or disturbing experience that can have long-lasting effects on an individual's mental and physical well-being. Examples of trauma include experiencing or witnessing violence, natural disasters, sexual or physical abuse, and accidents. Trauma can also be cumulative, resulting from multiple small events that add up over time.

When an individual experiences trauma, it can have a profound impact on their mental and emotional state. They may experience symptoms such as anxiety, depression, and flashbacks, which can make it difficult to function in daily life. Trauma can also disrupt the body's stress response, leading to chronic physical symptoms such as headaches, chronic pain, and stomach problems.

Substance abuse, on the other hand, is the use of drugs or alcohol in a way that is harmful to the individual or those around them. This can include using a substance in a way that is not medically prescribed, using a substance for longer than intended, or using a substance despite knowing it is causing problems in their life. Substance abuse can lead to addiction, a chronic brain disease characterized by compulsive drug-seeking and use despite the harmful consequences.

The relationship between trauma and substance abuse is complex and multifaceted. Trauma can lead to substance abuse as a way of coping with the overwhelming emotions and memories associated with the traumatic event. Drugs and alcohol can provide temporary relief from these symptoms, leading the individual to use them more frequently and eventually becoming addicted.

Additionally, individuals who have experienced trauma are

more likely to develop substance abuse problems than those who have not. Studies have shown that individuals who have experienced traumatic events are at a higher risk of developing substance abuse problems, with the risk increasing with the number of traumatic events experienced.

Substance abuse can also lead to further trauma. For example, individuals who are under the influence of drugs or alcohol may be more likely to be involved in accidents or violent incidents. Additionally, individuals who are addicted to drugs or alcohol may experience financial, legal, and relationship problems, which can also be traumatic.

Understanding the relationship between trauma and addiction is crucial in treating both conditions. Trauma-informed care is an approach that recognizes the impact of trauma and incorporates this understanding into the treatment process. This approach recognizes that individuals who have experienced trauma may have different needs and may require a different approach than those who have not.

Treatment for substance abuse typically includes a combination of therapy and medication. Therapy can include cognitive-behavioral therapy, which helps individuals identify and change negative thought patterns and behaviors associated with substance abuse. Medication-assisted treatment (MAT) can also be effective in treating substance abuse, particularly for individuals addicted to opioids.

Trauma-specific therapies, such as eye movement desensitization and reprocessing (EMDR) or prolonged exposure therapy, can also be effective in treating the symptoms of trauma. These therapies help individuals process and make sense of the traumatic event, reducing the emotional impact and allowing them to move forward.

In conclusion, trauma and addiction are closely intertwined and understanding the relationship between the two can aid in the treatment of both conditions. Trauma can lead to substance abuse as a way of coping with overwhelming emotions and memories. Substance abuse can also lead to further trauma, creating a cycle that can be difficult to break. Trauma-informed care, which recognizes the impact of trauma and incorporates this understanding into the treatment process, is crucial in treating both trauma and addiction. It is important to address both conditions simultaneously, as one can exacerbate the other.

It is also important to note that not all individuals who have experienced trauma will develop substance abuse problems, and not all individuals who struggle with substance abuse have a history of trauma. However, recognizing the potential connection between the two can aid in providing more comprehensive and effective treatment.

In addition to therapy and medication, other supportive measures such as self-care practices, mindfulness, and support groups can be beneficial in the treatment of trauma and addiction. A holistic approach that addresses physical, emotional, and social well-being can help individuals develop the skills and resilience to cope with difficult emotions and memories, and ultimately break the cycle of trauma and addiction.

It is important to remember that recovery from trauma and addiction is a journey, and it may take time for individuals to heal and recover. It is important to provide support and encouragement throughout the process and to remember that everyone's journey is unique. With the right approach and support, individuals can overcome the trauma and addiction and move forward towards a healthier and more ful-

12: TRAUMA AND ADDICTION: HOW TRAUMA CAN LEAD TO SUBSTANCE ABUSE

filling life.

13: Trauma and the Workplace: How Trauma Can Affect Your Career

Trauma is a deeply distressing or disturbing experience that can have a significant impact on an individual's mental and emotional well-being. Trauma can manifest in a variety of ways, including anxiety, depression, post-traumatic stress disorder (PTSD), and other mental health conditions. In this chapter, we will explore the ways in which trauma can affect an individual's career, including how it can impact job performance, relationships with colleagues and managers, and overall job satisfaction.

When an individual experiences trauma, it can affect their ability to focus and concentrate, making it difficult to complete tasks and meet deadlines. This can lead to decreased productivity and job performance, which can ultimately lead to disciplinary action or even termination. Additionally, trauma can cause individuals to struggle with maintaining healthy relationships with colleagues and managers, which can further impact their ability to succeed in their careers.

13: TRAUMA AND THE WORKPLACE: HOW TRAUMA CAN AFFECT YOUR CAREER

Trauma can also affect an individual's ability to cope with stress and handle difficult situations in the workplace. For example, an individual who has experienced trauma may struggle with handling criticism from a manager or dealing with a difficult customer. This can lead to increased absenteeism and high turnover rates, which can be detrimental to both the individual and the organization as a whole.

Furthermore, trauma can also affect an individual's ability to advance in their career. Those who have experienced trauma may struggle with networking, public speaking, and other important aspects of career development. This can make it difficult for individuals to secure promotions or move up in their organizations.

However, it is important to note that not all individuals who have experienced trauma will experience these negative effects in the workplace. Many people who have experienced trauma are able to successfully navigate their careers. Additionally, there are resources available to help individuals who are struggling with the effects of trauma in the workplace.

For example, employee assistance programs (EAPs) are

available to provide support and resources to employees who are struggling with mental health issues, including those related to trauma. These programs can provide counseling, therapy, and other forms of support to help employees cope with their experiences and improve their job performance.

Moreover, employers and managers can also play a role in supporting employees who have experienced trauma. This can include providing accommodations such as flexible schedules, additional time off, or changes to job duties. Additionally, managers and colleagues can be trained on how to recognize the signs of trauma and how to provide support to those who are struggling.

In conclusion, trauma can have a significant impact on an individual's career. It can affect job performance, relationships with colleagues and managers, and overall job satisfaction. However, with the right resources and support, individuals who have experienced trauma can successfully navigate their careers. Employers and managers can also play an important role in supporting employees who have experienced trauma and creating a more supportive and understanding work environment.

Another important aspect of addressing trauma in the workplace is creating a culture of openness and understanding. Many individuals who have experienced trauma may feel ashamed or embarrassed to talk about their experiences, which can further exacerbate the negative effects of trauma. By creating a culture where individuals feel safe and supported to talk about their experiences, employers and managers can help to mitigate the negative effects of trauma.

Additionally, employers can also provide training and education on trauma and its effects, for both employees and managers. This can help to increase understanding and awareness of the issue, and promote a more supportive and inclusive workplace.

It's also important to note that some individuals may require accommodations and support in order to function well in their jobs. These accommodations can include flexible work schedules, modified job duties, or additional time off for therapy and treatment. Employers should be willing to work with employees to provide these accommodations, as they can make a significant difference in helping individuals to manage the effects of trauma and be successful in their careers.

In summary, trauma can have a significant impact on an individual's career, but with the right resources and support, individuals can successfully navigate their careers. Employers and managers play an important role in creating a supportive and understanding work environment, and providing resources and support for employees who have experienced trauma. By creating a culture of openness and understanding, providing training and education, and offering accommodations, employers can help to mitigate the negative effects of trauma and promote a more inclusive and supportive workplace.

14: Trauma and the Legal System: Navigating the Challenges of Trauma and the Justice System

Trauma and the legal system can be a challenging and difficult topic to navigate. Trauma can affect individuals in a variety of ways and can have a significant impact on their ability to participate in the legal system. This chapter will explore the challenges of trauma and the justice system and provide strategies for navigating these challenges.

Trauma can be defined as a psychological response to a traumatic event or series of events. It can include symptoms such as anxiety, depression, and post-traumatic stress disorder (PTSD). Trauma can also affect an individual's cognitive abilities, including memory, attention, and decision-making. These symptoms can make it difficult for a person to participate in the legal system, particularly if they are a victim or witness in a criminal case.

Victims of trauma may have difficulty remembering details of the traumatic event or may be reluctant to talk about it. This can make it difficult for them to provide testimony in court or for prosecutors to build a strong case. Additionally, trauma can cause anxiety and distress, which can make it difficult for a victim to participate in court proceedings.

Trauma can also affect the way a person perceives and interprets events. This can make it difficult for them to understand legal proceedings and can also affect their ability to make decisions. For example, a victim of trauma may be hesitant to testify in court or may be unsure about whether to press charges against their abuser.

Trauma can also affect an individual's ability to participate in the legal system if they are a defendant in a criminal case. Trauma can affect an individual's decision-making and can also make it difficult for them to understand the legal proceedings. Additionally, trauma can cause anxiety and distress, which can make it difficult for a defendant to participate in court proceedings.

The criminal justice system can be a traumatic experience for victims, witnesses, and defendants. The legal process can be long and drawn out, and individuals may have to relive the traumatic event multiple times. Additionally, the criminal justice system can be a stressful and intimidating experience, particularly for individuals who have experienced trauma.

To navigate the challenges of trauma and the legal system, it is important to understand the impact of trauma and to work with professionals who are trained to support individuals who have experienced trauma. This can include working with therapists, counselors, and other mental health professionals.

Victims and witnesses of trauma may also benefit from advocacy services that provide support and guidance throughout the legal process. These services can help individuals understand the legal proceedings and can also provide emotional support. Additionally, victims and witnesses may benefit from participating in support groups or other forms of peer support.

For defendants who have experienced trauma, it is important to work with attorneys who are familiar with the impact of trauma and who can provide support and guidance throughout the legal process. Additionally, defendants may benefit from working with mental health professionals who can provide support and treatment for trauma.

It is also important for the legal system to take into account the impact of trauma when making decisions about criminal cases. This can include providing accommodations for victims and witnesses who have experienced trauma and taking into account the impact of trauma when determining sentences for defendants.

In conclusion, trauma and the legal system can be a challenging and difficult topic to navigate. Trauma can affect individuals in a variety of ways and can have a significant impact on their ability to participate in the legal system. To navigate these challenges, it is important to understand the impact of trauma and to work with professionals who are trained to support individuals who have experienced trauma. Additionally, it is important for the legal system to take into account the impact of trauma when making decisions about criminal cases.

Another important aspect to consider when navigating the challenges of trauma and the legal system is the role of trauma-informed practice. Trauma-informed practice involves understanding the impact of trauma on individuals and adapting the legal system to better serve those who have experienced trauma. This can include training for legal professionals on the effects of trauma, creating a more welcoming and understanding environment in courtrooms, and using language that is sensitive to the needs of trauma survivors.

Additionally, it is important for legal professionals to understand the intersectionality of trauma. Individuals who have experienced trauma may also have other marginalized identities, such as being a person of color or being a member of the LGBTQ+ community. These identities can compound the effects of trauma and can also affect an individual's experiences within the legal system. Therefore, it is important for legal professionals to be aware of and sensitive to the intersectionality of trauma.

Another key aspect of navigating the challenges of trauma and the legal system is understanding the role of restorative justice. Restorative justice is an approach to justice that focuses on repairing harm caused by crime and working with victims, offenders, and the community to find solutions that are fair and healing. This approach can be particularly beneficial for individuals who have experienced trauma, as it can provide them with a sense of empowerment and agency in the legal process.

In order to effectively navigate the challenges of trauma and the legal system, it is essential for individuals, legal professionals, and the legal system as a whole to work together. This includes understanding the impact of trauma, providing support and accommodations for individuals who have experienced trauma, and implementing trauma-informed practices within the legal system. Only by taking a holistic approach can we truly address the challenges of trauma and the legal system and ensure that justice is served for all.

In conclusion, trauma and the legal system can be a difficult and challenging topic to navigate. Trauma can have a significant impact on an individual's ability to participate in the legal system and can also affect the way in which legal decisions are made. To navigate these challenges, it is important for individuals, legal professionals, and the legal system as a whole to understand the impact of trauma and to implement trauma-informed practices. Additionally, a holistic approach that considers restorative justice and intersectionality of trauma is essential for providing a fair and healing justice system for all.

15: Trauma and the Impact on Children and Families

Trauma is an event or series of events that causes significant harm or distress to an individual or group of individuals. The effects of trauma can be long-lasting and have a profound impact on the mental and physical well-being of those affected. Children and families are particularly vulnerable to the effects of trauma, as they are often unable to understand or cope with the traumatic event.

Trauma can take many forms, including physical, emotional, and sexual abuse, neglect, natural disasters, and exposure to violence. Children and families who experience trauma may display a wide range of symptoms, including anxiety, depression, post-traumatic stress disorder (PTSD), and behavioral problems. These symptoms can have a significant impact on a child's ability to form healthy relationships, perform well in school, and function in other areas of life.

Children who have experienced trauma may have difficulty trusting others, feel detached or detached from their emotions, and experience flashbacks or nightmares related to the traumatic event. They may also exhibit aggressive or self-destructive behavior, such as fighting or substance abuse. These symptoms can be difficult to recognize and understand, and can be misinterpreted as disciplinary or behavioral issues rather than symptoms of trauma.

Families who have experienced trauma may also have difficulty functioning as a unit. Parents may struggle with their own mental health issues, including depression and PTSD, and may have difficulty providing the emotional support and stability that their children need. They may also have difficulty communicating with each other or with their children, which can further complicate the healing process.

It's important to recognize that trauma does not discriminate and can happen to anyone, regardless of race, socio-economic status, or other factors. It's also important to note that trauma can have a cumulative effect, meaning that even small traumas can add up over time and have a significant impact on a child's mental and emotional well-being.

Treatment for trauma can take many forms, including therapy, medication, and support groups. It's important to find a treatment that is tailored to the specific needs of the child and family. Trauma-focused cognitive behavioral therapy

(TF-CBT) is a form of therapy that has been shown to be effective in treating children and families who have experienced trauma. TF-CBT is a short-term, structured therapy that focuses on helping children and families understand and process their traumatic experiences, and learn new coping strategies to deal with the symptoms of trauma.

In addition to therapy, medication can also be an effective treatment for trauma-related symptoms, such as anxiety and depression. Medication should always be used in conjunction with therapy and should be prescribed by a qualified mental health professional.

Support groups can also be an important part of the healing process for children and families who have experienced trauma. Support groups provide a safe and supportive environment where children and families can share their experiences, learn from others, and receive support and encouragement.

It's important to remember that healing from trauma is a process and it can take time. Children and families may experience setbacks and may need to revisit certain topics or issues as they continue to heal. It's important to be patient and understanding, and to provide ongoing support and encouragement.

In conclusion, trauma can have a significant and lasting impact on children and families. It's important to recognize the symptoms of trauma and to provide appropriate treatment and support. With the right care and support, children and families can heal and move forward with their lives.

It's also important to remember that trauma does not only affect the individual who experienced it, but it also affects the entire family. Children and families often have to navigate the aftermath of trauma together, and it's essential to provide support and resources to the entire family unit.

Another important aspect of trauma is the recognition of its intergenerational effects. Trauma can be passed down from one generation to another, as parents who have experienced trauma may have difficulty providing a stable and safe environment for their children. This can lead to cycles of trauma and can make it harder for future generations to heal and move on from traumatic experiences.

Additionally, it's essential to understand that trauma can

have different effects on different people, even within the same family. Each person's experience and response to trauma are unique and should be acknowledged and respected.

Prevention is also an important aspect of addressing trauma. It's crucial to educate communities and families about the signs and effects of trauma, as well as providing resources and support to individuals and families who may be at risk of experiencing trauma.

In order to address the impact of trauma on children and families, it's essential to have a comprehensive approach that involves multiple sectors such as healthcare, education, social services, and criminal justice. Collaboration between these sectors is crucial in order to provide the appropriate support and resources for children and families affected by trauma.

In summary, trauma can have a lasting and profound impact on children and families. It's essential to recognize the symptoms of trauma, provide appropriate treatment and support, and address the intergenerational and systemic factors that contribute to the effects of trauma. By providing the necessary resources and support, children and families can heal and move forward with their lives.

16: Trauma and Spirituality: How Trauma Can Affect Faith and Beliefs

Trauma and spirituality are often intertwined, as individuals may turn to their faith or beliefs for comfort and understanding during difficult times. However, trauma can also have a profound impact on one's spirituality, potentially leading to feelings of betrayal, abandonment, and loss of meaning.

When an individual experiences trauma, they may question the belief that they previously held in a higher power or the concept of a benevolent universe. They may feel that their faith has been tested and found wanting, leading to feelings of anger and resentment towards their religion or belief system. Trauma can also lead to a loss of trust in the world and in others, making it difficult for an individual to connect with a higher power or find solace in spiritual practices.

Additionally, some individuals may feel that their faith or beliefs were responsible for their trauma, either through the actions of a religious leader or institution, or through the belief that they were being punished for their sins. This can lead to feelings of betrayal and abandonment, and may cause an individual to distance themselves from their faith or beliefs.

On the other hand, some individuals may find that their faith or beliefs provide them with a sense of strength and resilience during times of trauma. They may find comfort in the idea that their suffering has a greater purpose or that they are being tested in order to become a stronger person. They may also find solace in religious or spiritual practices, such as prayer, meditation, or connecting with a community of believers.

However, it's important to note that for some individuals, connecting with their faith or belief system may be challenging, and that's okay. Trauma can change us and our ways of thinking, and it's possible that an individual may find that they no longer identify with the religion or belief system they once held. It's important for individuals to allow themselves the space and time to process their experiences and to find meaning and purpose in their own way.

In summary, trauma can have a significant impact on an individual's spirituality, potentially leading to feelings of betrayal, abandonment, and loss of meaning. However, it's important to remember that different people have different ways of coping with trauma and finding meaning, and that it's important to respect and support an individual's unique journey.

It's also important for individuals who are struggling with the effects of trauma on their spirituality to seek out professional help. A therapist or counselor who is trained in trauma-informed care can provide support and guidance as an individual navigates the complex emotions and beliefs that may arise from their experiences. They can also help an individual develop coping strategies and resilience, and may provide referrals to support groups or other resources that can be beneficial.

Additionally, it can be helpful for individuals to explore other forms of spirituality or religion that may resonate with them more after experiencing trauma. For example, some individuals may find that nature-based spirituality or mindfulness practices provide a sense of peace and connection that traditional religions no longer do. It's important for individuals to explore different paths and find what works best for them.

It's also important to remember that healing from trauma is a process and it doesn't happen overnight. It may take time for an individual to come to terms with the trauma they have experienced and how it has affected their spirituality. It's important to be patient and compassionate with oneself and to take the time needed to heal.

In conclusion, trauma can have a significant impact on an individual's spirituality, but it's important to remember that healing is possible and that different paths may be taken to find meaning and purpose. It's essential to seek professional help, explore different spiritual practices, and be patient with oneself in the healing process. Remember that healing is a journey, not a destination, and that it's important to be gentle with oneself during this time.

17: Moving Forward: Finding Purpose and Meaning After Trauma

Trauma can be a devastating and life-altering event. It can leave us feeling lost, confused, and without a sense of purpose or direction. But it is important to remember that healing is possible, and that we can move forward and find meaning and purpose in our lives again.

The first step in moving forward after trauma is to acknowledge and accept that it has happened. Denying or suppressing the trauma will only prolong the healing process. It is important to give yourself time and space to grieve and process the emotions that come with the trauma. This may include seeking support from a therapist or counselor, or joining a support group for people who have experienced similar trauma.

Once you have begun to process the trauma, it is important to focus on self-care. This includes taking care of your physical, emotional, and mental well-being. Eating a healthy diet, getting enough sleep, and regular exercise can all help to promote healing. It is also important to find healthy ways to cope with stress and anxiety, such as through mindfulness practices like meditation or yoga.

17: MOVING FORWARD: FINDING PURPOSE AND MEANING AFTER TRAUMA

As you begin to heal, it is also important to find ways to integrate the trauma into your life. This may include finding meaning in the experience, such as by using it to help others who have experienced similar trauma. It may also involve finding a new sense of purpose or direction in life. This may involve returning to school or starting a new career, or simply finding ways to give back to your community.

Another important aspect of moving forward after trauma is to focus on building and maintaining positive relationships. Surrounding yourself with supportive and understanding people can provide much-needed emotional support and encouragement during this difficult time. It is also important to find ways to connect with others who have experienced similar trauma, as this can help to provide a sense of validation and understanding.

As you continue to heal and move forward, it is important to remember that healing is not a linear process. There may be setbacks and triggers that cause the trauma to feel fresh again. It is important to be patient with yourself and to understand that healing takes time. It is also important to remember that it is not necessary to achieve a state of complete healing in order to move forward and find purpose and meaning in life again.

In conclusion, moving forward after trauma can be a difficult and challenging process, but it is possible. By acknowledging and accepting the trauma, focusing on self-care, finding ways to integrate the trauma into your life, building positive relationships, and being patient with yourself, you can begin to heal and find purpose and meaning in your life again. Remember to reach out for help, be kind to yourself and don't give up hope.

It's important to know that healing is a personal journey, what works for one person may not work for another, so be open to explore different options and different paths. It's also important to remind yourself that trauma does not define you and you are capable of overcoming it and finding a new path in life.

Another important aspect of moving forward after trauma is to focus on the present and the future, rather than dwelling on the past. This may involve setting goals for yourself and working towards them, whether they are related to your career, personal relationships, or personal growth. By setting and achieving goals, you can begin to regain a sense of control over your life and a sense of purpose.

It may also be helpful to engage in activities that bring you joy and fulfillment. This can include hobbies, volunteer work, or other interests that you are passionate about. Engaging in activities that you enjoy can help to take your mind off of the trauma and provide a sense of accomplishment and satisfaction.

Another important aspect of moving forward after trauma is to focus on forgiveness. Forgiveness is not about forgetting or excusing the actions of the person or event that caused the trauma, but rather about letting go of the anger and resentment that can hold us back. Forgiving the person or event can help to release the emotional burden and move forward in a positive direction.

In addition, it's important to learn from the trauma and use it as an opportunity for personal growth. Trauma can be a powerful teacher that can help us to develop resilience, empathy, and a deeper understanding of ourselves and others. This can give us a new perspective on life and open up new opportunities for growth and self-discovery.

17: MOVING FORWARD: FINDING PURPOSE AND MEANING AFTER TRAUMA

Moving forward after trauma can be a difficult and challenging journey, but it is not impossible. With patience, self-care, and a focus on the present and future, it is possible to heal and find purpose and meaning in life again. Remember to reach out for help, be kind to yourself and don't give up hope.

It's important to remember that healing is not a destination, it's a process, and it's not a one-time event. It's a continuous journey that requires effort and commitment. You may stumble or fall down, but you can always get back up and keep moving forward.

In conclusion, Moving forward after trauma is a process that requires effort and commitment. By acknowledging and accepting the trauma, focusing on self-care, finding ways to integrate the trauma into your life, building positive relationships, setting goals and focusing on the present and future, forgiveness, and learning from the trauma, you can begin to heal and find purpose and meaning in your life again. Remember to reach out for help, be kind to yourself and don't give up hope.

18: Conclusion: The Importance of Continuing Support and Self-Discovery in Trauma Recovery

Trauma recovery is a lifelong process that requires ongoing support and self-discovery. The road to healing from trauma can be difficult and bumpy, but with the right support and resources, individuals can learn to manage their symptoms and live fulfilling lives.

The importance of continuing support in trauma recovery cannot be overstated. Trauma survivors often struggle with feelings of isolation and shame, and may not feel comfortable reaching out for help. It is crucial that they have access to a supportive community, whether that be in the form of therapy, support groups, or loved ones. Having a safe space to process and share their experiences can help individuals feel less alone and more understood.

In addition to ongoing support, self-discovery is also crucial in trauma recovery. Trauma can leave individuals feeling disconnected from themselves and their emotions. Through self-discovery, individuals can learn to understand and accept their experiences and emotions, rather than repressing or denying them. This can lead to greater self-awareness and self-compassion, which can help individuals build a more resilient and fulfilling life.

There are many different forms of therapy that can help individuals in their trauma recovery journey. Cognitive Behavioral Therapy (CBT) is one of the most widely-used evidence-based therapies and can help individuals learn to manage their symptoms and improve their overall well-being. Eye Movement Desensitization and Reprocessing (EMDR) is a therapy that can help individuals process traumatic memories and reduce symptoms of trauma such as anxiety, depression, and nightmares. Other therapies such as Mindfulness-Based Stress Reduction (MBSR) and yoga can also be beneficial for trauma recovery.

In addition to traditional therapy, alternative forms of healing such as art therapy, music therapy, and journaling can also be helpful for trauma survivors. These forms of therapy can provide individuals with a creative outlet for expressing their emotions, which can be especially beneficial for those who may not feel comfortable verbalizing their experiences.

18: CONCLUSION: THE IMPORTANCE OF CONTINUING SUPPORT AND SELF-DISCOVERY IN TRAUMA RECOVERY

It is important to note that trauma recovery is not always linear and individuals may experience setbacks. It is important to understand that healing is a process and it can take time. It is also important to note that everyone is different and there is no "one size fits all" approach to trauma recovery. Some individuals may find that traditional therapy works best for them, while others may find that alternative forms of healing are more beneficial.

In conclusion, trauma recovery is a lifelong process that requires ongoing support and self-discovery. Having access to a supportive community and various forms of therapy can help individuals manage their symptoms and improve their overall well-being. Remember that healing is a process and everyone is different, so it is important to find what works best for you.

It is also important for individuals to understand that healing from trauma is not just about managing symptoms, but also about learning to live a fulfilling life. This can involve setting and achieving personal goals, building healthy relationships, and finding a sense of purpose. Trauma recovery can also involve learning to accept and forgive oneself for past experiences and mistakes, as well as learning to let go of negative thoughts and beliefs about oneself.

For some individuals, trauma recovery may also involve facing and addressing the root cause of their trauma. This may involve seeking justice for past injustices, such as filing a report or pressing charges against an abuser. It may also involve addressing systemic issues, such as advocating for policy changes or participating in activism.

It is also important to understand that trauma recovery is not just the responsibility of the individual. As a society, we must work to create a culture of understanding and support for trauma survivors. This includes educating ourselves about the effects of trauma, being aware of the signs of trauma in others, and being willing to offer help and support when needed. It also includes working to eliminate the root causes of trauma, such as poverty, racism, and discrimination.

In conclusion, trauma recovery is a lifelong process that requires ongoing support, self-discovery, and a commitment to living a fulfilling life. It is important to understand that

18: CONCLUSION: THE IMPORTANCE OF CONTINUING SUPPORT AND SELF-DISCOVERY IN TRAUMA RECOVERY

everyone's journey is unique, and it is essential to find the right forms of therapy and support that work best for the individual. As a society, we must also strive to create a culture of understanding and support for trauma survivors, and work towards eliminating the root causes of trauma. Remember that healing is possible and with the right support, individuals can learn to manage their symptoms, and live fulfilling lives.

Thank You

As we reach the end of this book, I want to say thanks for reading this book.

I want to get this information out to as many people as possible. If you found this book helpful, I would greatly appreciate you leaving me a review. This helps others find the book as well.

Disclaimer

This document is geared towards providing exact and reliable information in regards to the topic and issue covered. The publication is sold on the idea that the publisher is not required to render an accounting, officially permitted, or otherwise, qualified services. If advice is necessary, legal, financial, medical or professional, a practiced individual in the profession should be ordered.

This information is not presented by a financial or medical practitioner and is for entertainment, educational and informational purposes only. The content is not intended as a substitute for professional medical advice, diagnosis, or treatment. Always seek the advice of your physician or other qualified health care provider with any questions you may have regarding a medical condition. Never disregard professional medical advice or delay in seeking it because of something you have read.

The information provided herein is stated to be truthful and consistent, in that any liability, in terms of inattention or otherwise, by any usage or abuse of any policies, processes, or directions contained within is the solitary and utter responsibility of the recipient reader. Under no circumstances

DISCLAIMER

will any legal responsibility or blame be held against the publisher for any reparation, damages, or monetary loss due to the information herein, either directly or indirectly.

www.ingramcontent.com/pod-product-compliance
Lightning Source LLC
Chambersburg PA
CBHW060513130626
46553CB00002B/484

* 9 7 9 8 8 8 9 1 3 0 5 0 5 *